Praise for *Shattering Inequities: Real-World Wisdom for School and District Leaders*

"*Shattering Inequities* is written for educational leaders with the courage and readiness to expose those systemic practices and mindsets that betray the promise of educational equality for students from historically disenfranchised communities. The reader profits from what we've learned from academic research, combined with the authors' years of on-the-ground experience working in schools. Avelar La Salle and Johnson provide a myriad of proven strategies for imagining and instituting new practices that enable all students to achieve academic success. The text is consistently engaging, replete with brainy concepts, metaphors, and moral imperatives that simultaneously enlighten, inspire, and instruct."—**Ricardo D. Stanton-Salazar**, PhD, author, *Manufacturing Hope & Despair*, The School and Kin Support Networks of U.S.-Mexican Youth

"I believe that all educators come to their work to make a difference for the children who need us the most. Holding that desire in your heart is a necessary condition, but alone will not make a difference. It takes thoughtful, strategic, and deliberate action to accomplish this. Robin and Ruth give you a roadmap with proven paths to turn your good intentions into reality for the children you serve. You simply add courage and determination. If you can only read one book this year, read this one."—**Laura Schwalm**, retired superintendent, Garden Grove School District, and senior partner, California Education Partners

"*Shattering Inequities* is jammed with real world solutions based on everyday, real world problems for anyone who wants to make a difference in the lives of students. This book sizzles with practical, doable lessons for all of us equity leaders who demand educational justice for our most vulnerable students. Avelar La Salle and Johnson's well-researched book should be required reading for all school staff and district leaders who work in school districts who serve students of color and/or low-income students. They are absolutely correct—*'Enough is enough.'* Those of us who call ourselves 'educators' have a moral imperative to implement these positive solutions in our classrooms, schools, and districts."—**Paula Crisostomo**, assistant dean of students for intercultural affairs, emeritus, Occidental College, and student leader of the 1968 East L.A. High School Walkouts

"Having followed the work of Drs. Avelar LaSalle and Johnson, I approached their manuscript with enthusiasm. I knew *Shattering Inequities* would be relevant, approachable, and timeless. I met Kyle in the Preface. We all know 'Kyles' who have been poorly served in our schools. This book takes the energy bound up in educator frustration with social and institutional inequities and equips the reader with the means to engage self and colleagues in learning how to educate all children and youth. Equitable education is portrayed as an inside-out process that engages educators and school systems to embrace shared values and beliefs in which equity is a moral imperative."—**Randall B. Lindsey**, coauthor, *Cultural Proficiency: A Manual for School Leaders*

"From a historical and topical view, there is a mountain of evidence to conclude that schooling in the United States is a system and structure purposely designed to produce inequalities. To counter or even *shatter* such contrived arrangements, there is a need for a systemic approach that especially gives primacy to school leaders. *Shattering Inequities: Real-World Wisdom for School and District Leaders* by Robin Avelar La Salle and Ruth S. Johnson does just that. It provides educational leaders with the most plausible, clear, and measurable methods to produce equitable schools."—**Dr. Nana Lawson Bush, V**, professor of educational leadership and pan-African studies at California State University, Los Angeles, and author, *The Plan: A Guide for Women Raising African American Boys from Conception to College*

"The authors have their fingers on the pulse of the injustices that plague our educational system beginning with the heart-wrenching story about Kyle. They are relentless in not only identifying the problems, but offer real life examples, analysis, and solutions for reducing inequities that exist. The book requires that each of us summon the courage within and take action to do right by our children, especially those who have been histori-cally underserved by an inequitable antiquated system."—**Brenda Campbell Jones**, PhD, CEO, *CampbellJones & Associates*, and coauthor, *The Culturally Proficient Journey: Moving Beyond Ethical Barriers Toward Profound School Change*

"As educators, we have a moral imperative to support all students. Yet, we don't always have the strong models that we can turn to for inspiration. Robin and Ruth simplify the theoretical knowledge into practical steps that help practitioners use data to reflect on current practices and develop a systematic action-oriented approach to support all students. Through these shared lessons, educators can move forward with confidence know-ing that they are not alone in fighting inequities. They now can transform their passion and love for students into successful equity actions."—**Gudiel Crosthwaite**, PhD, super-intendent, Lynwood Unified School District, Lynwood, California

"At last, a solution that guarantees that kids get what they need and deserve. Should everyone embrace the strategies and courage needed to do the work recommended in the reading, we won't have to worry about educational gaps any longer."—**Paul Gothold**, superintendent, San Diego County Office of Education

Shattering Inequities

Shattering Inequities

*Real-World Wisdom for
School and District Leaders*

Robin Avelar La Salle
Ruth S. Johnson

ROWMAN & LITTLEFIELD
Lanham • Boulder • New York • London

Published by Rowman & Littlefield
An imprint of The Rowman & Littlefield Publishing Group, Inc.
4501 Forbes Boulevard, Suite 200, Lanham, Maryland 20706
www.rowman.com

6 Tinworth Street, London, SE11 5AL, United Kingdom

British Library Cataloguing in Publication Information Available

Library of Congress Cataloging-in-Publication Data Available

ISBN 9781475844160 (cloth: alk. paper) | IBSN 9781475844177 (pbk. : alk. paper) | ISBN 9781475844184 (electronic)

♾ ™ The paper used in this publication meets the minimum requirements of American National Standard for Information Sciences Permanence of Paper for Printed Library Materials, ANSI/NISO Z39.48-1992.

Printed in the United States of America

To all people who believe that every student is entitled to the premium education that only some currently experience.

Contents

Foreword

Shattering Inequities is a stunning book—in its courage, precision, relentless problem solving, and utter clarity. It tackles the most devastating problem of the day facing our school system and society as a whole: the growing and towering inequality of performance that is endemic in our public school systems. No one has laid out and dissected the array of inequity problems so clearly; no one has systematically dealt with each problem so convincingly. No one has identified every aspect of inequity with such exposition; no one has dealt with each problem with such dispatch.

Robin Avelar La Salle and Ruth Johnson have done the seemingly impossible. They don't underestimate the apparent intractability of attacking inequity, but somehow they show and make the reader believe that "this phenomenon" (reducing inequity) is decidedly possible. Each chapter is succinct and powerfully action oriented. Every solution and action in the book—successful or not—is based on real people in real solutions. By the end of the book there are no hypotheticals.

They start with moral imperative, but it is not the lofty pronouncements that they feature. They treat moral imperative as a credibility phenomenon. No nonsense from the get-go: "assume that inequities exist"; examine microdata (the performance of all subgroups); "look for trouble" in all the right places; "see yourself as someone who is personally responsible for fixing the situation" and embrace "the power of assuming that inequities exist crystallizes the role of an equity educational leader in actionable terms." Pay attention to the fringes and make equity for all a reality. All this is the moral imperative.

Chapter 2 makes "data the equity engine." Every chapter hooks the reader with a series of "have you ever wondered . . ." statements such as:

- "How comfortable do you or others feel when people discuss data?"
- "Do you have the expertise to use data as an equity tool?"
- "Why don't reports always match what you perceive to be true in your school or district?"

The authors use the "wallpaper" metaphor throughout the book. When is "wallpaper magic" used to cover up less attractive realities? How can you uncover and do something about deeply rooted systemic inequities in school systems?

Chapter 3 discusses what to do when one or more adults are the problem. How do you confront such problems in a way that results in improvement? Each chapter identifies and discusses equity concepts and equity actions. In this case—problematic adults—we learn how *leadership maturity, leadership grace*, and *leadership responsiveness* operate, and how certain equity actions—find the love, demonstrate empathy, situate yourself inside the problem, and share your own story—move the situation forward.

Chapter 4 takes us to the heart of addressing any complex change problem: motivation. The authors ask: Have you ever wondered about what is the most effective way of inspiring people to act on an equity proposal, what are the least effective ways, and why do people not agree on what is true even in the face of data and facts? Then come the solutions: demonstrate humility; build on prior success; shine a light on relatable models; grow methodically.

What about "building an equity culture"? In chapter 5 we encounter a leader who tried everything to invite his teachers to address a growing equity situation but got nowhere until he said, "I want you to want to"—leading staff to figure out the way forward with the leader. The equity actions include presume positive intentions, when you get stumped think aloud, try on their shoes, and make sure you can walk in their new shoes.

Chapter 6 shows the reader how to identify, examine, and use "the power of expectations." The authors show us how to become fluent in equity language, how to use data-derived language, how to build need-based support models, and how to establish and monitor aggressive student outcome goals. "Never plan for modest growth," say the authors; "establish aggressive goals in a fixed time period." The authors are direct in their toughest questions and responses: What conditions would be necessary for a student who is well behind to reach grade level in two years? What are the liabilities of labeling, poor expectations, and hidden belief systems? Getting fluent in equity language and actions such as "establish and monitor aggressive student outcome goals" is the answer.

Chapter 7 confronts the most difficult set of issues: setting the conditions for building collective equity. It tells the story of a leader who entered as a leader in a system where there were some good things happening, along with hidden failures that went unnoticed. Somehow the leader fell on the theme

"A star does not a constellation make." Then came the telling actions: create an equity map, define equitable outcomes, define the acceptable floor, celebrate constellations, and create a progress monitoring system.

Chapter 8 starts by identifying five common mistakes, including "more is better," "trusting without verifying," and "privileging adult interests over student needs."

The conclusion of the book is that there is a very large *potential* community out there that has an equity heart. They just haven't figured out "the know-how to lead with equity actions." But this is only potential; who knows if they really have the courage and the heart to engage in and pursue a very tough battle for equity outcomes in the face of deeply rooted, hurtful systemic values and cultures that have been on a relentless rise for the past half century. I do know one way we can test this possibility: Have your community engage in an action-study group with this book as the weapon, with the sole and determined purpose to shatter your own ceiling of inequity, and prove that it can be done. Avelar La Salle and Johnson "want you to want to"!

Michael Fullan
Author and Consultant

Preface

Is this book for you? Read the following story of an actual student and then decide.

Kyle was never a star student, but he got by. A quiet and shy boy, he managed to get passed from grade to grade without much notice. He realized early on that if he just stayed out of trouble and turned assignments in, his teachers would be satisfied and he could earn Cs on his report cards. He was the second of three children who lived with their mother in a small rural town. His mom left school early to start working and was pleased that her son was doing fine in school.

When Kyle was in third grade, his teacher told his mother that he would be participating in a morning math program. Kyle did not hate math—he did not hate, or love, any subject—so he dutifully attended. He played some computer games each morning, with little interaction with the teacher's aide who opened the door when he and ten other students arrived every day.

In the fifth grade, Kyle was assigned to a new teacher and was pleased to see that the ten morning students were in his class. He was not asked to come to school early that year. Instead, the teacher told his mom that Kyle's teacher would be using a special math program in class for all of her students. Kyle thought nothing of it since all his classmates had the same book. He noticed that his cousin, who was in another fifth-grade classroom, had a different math book. His cousin's book was newer.

After a long summer, Kyle started middle school. He reported to the office the first day and received his class schedule. He was pleased to see history listed as his first-period class. He had secretly enjoyed learning about American history in the fifth grade. He was one of the only students to memorize the Preamble to the Constitution, though he never let on to his teacher that he had learned it. He was also fascinated whenever he saw replicas of actual historical documents, such as John Hancock's original signature and old photos. He was especially interested in the government, how the first president came to be, and how people get elected to office.

He got to first period and was relieved to see many familiar faces of students who had been in his fifth-grade class. He sat down next to them and shared their slightly bewildered first-day-of-middle-school looks. As he moved through his day, he noticed that most of his friends were in all of his classes—what a relief!

His last period was math. His teacher seemed kind and explained that they were lucky. This class was an "easy A" because they would be reviewing fifth-grade math. She passed out the books and Kyle noticed that it looked a lot like the math book his cousin used the year before, but it was brand new. He would make sure to use a book cover to keep it nice all year.

Kyle's middle school experience seemed okay. He learned that grades matter to people much more in middle school and that "passing" was anything above an F. So Kyle was "passing" middle school. Still on the shy side, he wanted to play a little sports at school, or maybe join the history club, or the future teachers club (maybe he'd like to teach history one day), but none of his friends were involved in those activities, and he felt uncomfortable around unfamiliar people.

So he just went to school every day, turned in homework, and continued to pass his classes. As he crossed the stage at the eighth-grade promotion ceremony, Kyle imagined what high school would be like and decided that it would be different. He decided to tell his high school counselor about his secret interest in history and his idea about becoming a history teacher— maybe he could teach at his own middle school. Maybe he would even run for a student body office. That would be something!

The first day of high school, Kyle reported to the office for his class schedule. He was confused to see that he had no history class. He had all the regular subjects, and two electives called Life Skills and High School Success, but no history. While that was disappointing, he was comforted to see so many familiar faces in his classes throughout the day. His sixth-period math class was interesting.

The teacher was young and energetic. This was his first teaching job and he was very happy to be at that school. Kyle knew that ninth-graders at his high school took algebra. His book was called Readiness for Algebra. His cousin's book was called Algebra: College-Prep, but algebra is algebra, he guessed.

At the end of the ninth grade, Kyle received a call slip to see his counselor. His counselor seemed very nice. Since he was passing all of his classes, Kyle intended to tell her about his interest in history, his plans for a career in teaching, and his hopes of running for school office in the spring.

Before he got a chance, the counselor told him that she was meeting with all students who were at risk of not graduating—not graduating! She told him that many students like him in the Title I program . . . what program? . . . with a history of poor test scores . . . huh? . . . often had trouble passing the high school graduation exam . . . you have to pass a test to graduate from high school? She was also worried that he might not complete the required high school coursework for graduation unless he attended summer school each year.

As it turns out, Kyle was on a different track from other students. Though he never realized it (but in retrospect, he had suspected), Kyle had trouble in math as early as second grade. As a result, he was identified Title I, which meant the school had to give him extra support. Also, because his family sometimes spoke Spanish at home, he was considered an English learner (EL) and had to get extra help for that, too. Even though Kyle almost never spoke Spanish himself, this label put him into certain classes and kept him out of others.

The morning program was supposed to provide that extra support and close his math and EL gap, but it did not. His elementary school grouped all the fifth-grade Title I students into one class to provide them extra support. That was supposed to close the gap, but it did not. The middle school placed students in pathways based on fifth-grade test scores, so Kyle and the other at-risk students were grouped together for math, which, by virtue of master scheduling constraints, grouped them together most of the day. This also satisfied the requirement that EL students be grouped. Teachers received rosters of their identified students and modified their curriculum and expectations to the level of the class with the intent of helping students be more successful. Kyle's name was on those lists. That was supposed to close the gap, but it did not.

Finally, the high school used test scores and teacher recommendations for placement in ninth-grade courses. Based on his middle school record, Kyle was placed in less rigorous courses. To make room for those helper classes, history was deferred that year.

That day with the counselor, Kyle learned that biology and chemistry were required courses, but that he could not take them until he took algebra and geometry. It turned out that algebra prep didn't count for anything but elective credit. He learned that the high school graduation exam was administered to tenth graders and contained middle school and high school material that had never been covered in his classes. He saw that his electives and lower-level classes took up the spaces other students were using to graduate on time.

For the first time, he felt very out of place and different from other students. He let the counselor talk, count credits, show him summer school schedules and lists of courses, testing dates, and addresses of local continuation high schools and adult schools. When she finished, she asked if he had any questions. "No. Thank you," he replied.

As he left the office, he realized he had forgotten to mention that he loved history. Kyle attended summer school, was transferred to an alternative program, and then one day stopped going to school.

How do you feel after reading about Kyle's educational journey? Are you struggling to put words to your feelings, but know that something went terribly, terribly wrong for Kyle? Do you feel like the educational system let Kyle down? Are you reflecting on all the Kyles you've known over the years?

If so, read on.

WHY READ THIS BOOK?

We wrote this book for one reason: *We are beyond frustrated over national educational statistics that make it seem like demographics determine destiny.* Low-income and racial and ethnic minorities are still at the bottom of the American ladder in every way: health, employment, income, housing, nutrition, civic engagement, and *education.* This book provides educational leaders a set of essential equity concepts and key actions that can break the cycle of persistently poor outcomes for the same demographic groups of students that have always struggled in our educational system.

WHO WILL BENEFIT FROM THIS BOOK?

The lessons between the covers of this book fortify the ability of educational leaders to make equity-grounded decisions and inspire equity-driven action to transform student lives and change communities. This book is written for administrators, teachers, counselors, other school staff, and community leaders who care about equitable education systems. As educators wrestle with disrupting legacies of poor student outcomes, this book will become a practical and trusted companion, providing a catalog of easily retrievable equity illustrations that apply to real-life, everyday challenges.

How do we do the true, right, and just thing for all the Kyles? Turn the page.

Acknowledgments

We sincerely appreciate the constellation of people who inspired us and contributed their support and input to this book. The stories in the book are true; the names were changed, but you know who you are. We thank each of you for your equity leadership on behalf of our most vulnerable students. You inspire us.

Thank you to Michael Fullan for your encouragement and support for this project and especially for writing the foreword. We thank the Orenda Education team (formerly Principal's Exchange) for their involvement with the content and their feedback on drafts—you are models of what it means to be an equity leader. A special thank-you goes to Randy Barth, Sang Peruri, and the entire Think Together organization for their encouragement and collaboration on this project. Thank you also to Sandy Thorstenson for always reminding us that demographics do not determine destiny.

We send love to our family and friends for their enthusiasm and patience while we dedicated our time to this project. Our children and grandchildren continue to serve as an inspiration for us. Thank you, and we love each of you more than you will ever know.

We appreciate the technical and overall support from David La Salle, who in large ways and small was integral to our ability to complete the book. Martha Avelar—a true equity leader—we thank you for sharing your lessons with us. Also, Shawn Johnson deserves a special acknowledgment for her input on drafts and help clarifying our thinking.

Special thanks to Susan Hills for helping shape our thinking early on. We appreciate your generosity of spirit and excitement about our work. We appreciate you, Sarah Jubar, our acquisitions editor for Rowman & Littlefield. You encouraged and guided us through the publication process with skill and grace. Finally, we thank you, William Diepenbrock, for your skilled technical support on the manuscript.

Introduction

Every system is perfectly designed to get the results it gets. Give that some thought.

This book illustrates the systems in schools and districts that perpetuate historical and persistent underachievement for the same demographic groups of students who have struggled for decades. It provides educators with a set of specific lessons aimed at breaking through the long-standing educational glass ceiling that is mostly invisible but very real. For leaders who believe that *every* student—regardless of family circumstance or ZIP code—is entitled to the best education, this book will demonstrate how *your* leadership can bring about equitable outcomes for our most vulnerable students.

This book is for leaders, including teachers, administrators, counselors, other support staff, and anyone else who cares about ensuring that every child has access to a high-quality education. Equity-minded educators often feel alone in their perspectives and concerns. You are *not* alone. This book will validate you and help you feel like part of an equity community that shares your values and beliefs about the moral imperative to educate every child with the premium education that only some currently experience.

The examples shared in each chapter offer lessons from actual leaders in schools and districts who are committed to having educational equity be their True North.

- Educational equity is a measure of the fundamental fairness of a school or district system.
- True North is a fixed point on a world that constantly spins.

An Equity True North is a fixed ideal that educational leaders rely on to inform their daily practice in a way that ensures that every student has the opportunity to access the best schooling available anywhere and the support they need to succeed.

This book features examples of actual leaders in actual schools and districts. Only the names have been changed. Complex leadership lessons are shared as easily retrievable Equity Hooks. Equity Hooks function the same way as musical hooks in songs. Musical hooks are very memorable parts of songs that remind listeners of a whole song with just a line, a phrase, or a few notes. For example, what comes to mind when you read the following lyrics and think of the accompanying melodies?

1. It's now or never/Come hold me tight.
2. Turn the beat around/Love to hear percussion.
3. Rollin', rollin', rollin' on the river.
4. You are the sunshine of my life/That's why I'll always stay around.
5. You're mine and we belong together/Yes, we belong together, for eternity.

How many musical hooks connect with you? Do you remember the songs simply by reading the lyrics of the hook? What memories do you connect to these songs? Many of us remember some or all of the songs just by the few words in the hook, and even hear the melodies in our minds. (For those of you who cannot wait to know the "right answers," here they are: 1. Elvis Presley; 2. Gloria Estefan; 3. Tina Turner; 4. Stevie Wonder; 5. Richie Valens [Valenzuela].)

In like fashion, Equity Hooks are short quips or phrases that are easily remembered. They trigger recall of complex and nuanced equity leadership lessons shared between the covers of this book. The lessons inform equity-grounded decisions and inspire equity-driven actions that have the power to transform the lives of our most vulnerable students.

For leaders who wrestle with the challenges of disrupting legacies of poor student outcomes, this book will become a trusted companion, providing a catalog of essential equity concepts and effective equity actions that apply to real-life, everyday challenges. These lessons will provide leaders with thoughtful, reflective, and timely ways to address educational equity that will inform daily decisions and inspire impactful leadership.

The following graphic outlines three essential questions about equity leadership that serve as the structure of the book. In each part of the book, beginning from the core at the center of the graphic and then moving out, we share nuanced and complex leadership lessons that transcend conventional thinking. The lessons equip equity-minded leaders with specific and practical strategies for addressing systemic inequities in schools and districts.

Each chapter has a title and an Equity Hook subtitle to serve as the memory jogger for the larger scope of the chapter.

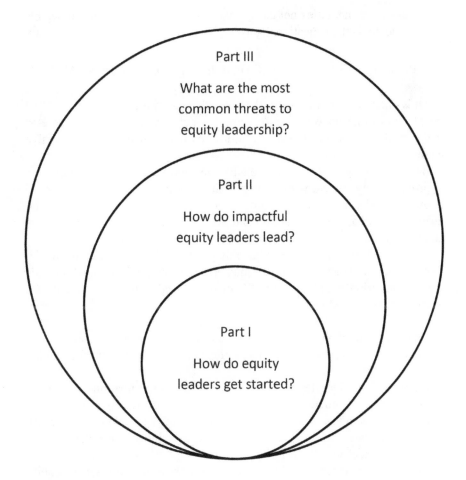

Figure I.1. Structure of the Book

PART I: HOW DO EQUITY LEADERS GET STARTED?

Who are equity leaders? What do equity leaders do, say, think, and feel? This part is a discussion of the core of figure I.1. Chapters 1 and 2 describe two key definers of equity leaders.

1. Equity leaders are guided by a moral imperative to ensure that every child receives the premium education that only some currently experience. Educational equity serves as their True North.
2. Equity leaders are keenly aware of, and proactively fight against, the risk of the *Wallpaper Effect*. That is, they ensure that they expose

systemic inequities not easily visible, but very harmful to vulnerable students—the educational glass ceiling.

PART II: HOW DO IMPACTFUL EQUITY LEADERS LEAD?

What is one thing—in the worst of times—that sustains equity leaders? Most people know the answer is *relationships*. Yet sometimes we struggle to understand how to develop the relationships that will build the collective equity muscle that points to Equity True North.

How do equity leaders motivate others to become engaged in the mission to provide every student with the premium education that only some currently experience? Leadership is only one side of a two-sided coin. Leaders who charge up a hill and then look around to find themselves alone are not leaders at all. They may have leadership titles, but they are not leaders.

A hallmark of equity leaders is that they inspire others to get in touch with their own equity heart and to take equity action. Chapters 3 through 7 provide a whirlwind trip through the work life of equity leaders who must work with adults so they can help students.

- Chapter 3 provides guidance on how to deal with hostility.
- Chapter 4 describes an effective strategy for working with challenging teams.
- Chapter 5 provides lessons about how to address situations where the ideas of adults around you do not match your Equity True North.
- Chapter 6 demonstrates a way to get underneath the words people use about students and families to identify the belief systems that lead to dangerous decisions for students.
- Chapter 7 provides valuable lessons about how to cultivate an equity culture focused on student success. It also describes an approach for dealing with inequitable practices that must be halted immediately, bypassing an extensive process.

PART III: WHAT ARE THE MOST COMMON THREATS TO EQUITY LEADERSHIP?

Part III provides lessons about how to skillfully navigate the many reactions people have when equity leaders propose change initiatives. In contrast, Part III describes the most common challenges equity leaders face when trying to follow their Equity True North, which are all within the control of the leaders. Chapter 8 describes the most common self-imposed hurdles to equity leadership. The chapter outlines the five most frequent mistakes that even experienced leaders make, and that too often stop good work right in its tracks.

With the stakes so high for our most vulnerable students, this chapter provides clear advice about how to avoid these bad calls so that the sincere efforts of equity leaders can translate into opportunity for and access to excellent schooling so that demographics *do not* determine destiny.

Part I

How Do Equity Leaders Get Started?

Chapter One

A Moral Imperative

Equity Hook: Go to Work and Look for Trouble

Have you ever wondered . . .

- What equity really means in education?
- What it means to be an "equity leader"?
- What the True North is that guides equity leaders?
- How leaders become equity leaders?
- What equity leaders do, say, think, feel, and accomplish?
- How equity leaders get started disrupting inequities?

Most educators do not make it their business to look for trouble. Yet a hard-working principal who was frustrated by a long history of poor student achievement for his population of vulnerable students learned the importance of doing just that. "Looking for trouble" was precisely what he was *not* doing and was missing.

Mr. Velarde was the principal of a large, complex elementary school in one of the highest-crime areas near a big city. Assigned five years prior, Mr. Velarde was responsible for more than one thousand K–5 students. About 80 percent were Latino and 20 percent were African American, mostly from working-class families. He also had a "spirited" staff of fifty, most of whom had been at the school for years.

During his time at the school, Mr. Velarde diligently addressed the many challenges that come with such a complex school and community. Parent, student, and neighborhood issues needed urgent attention on most days. He arrived every morning by 6:30, wanting to get ahead of anything that might disrupt the day, and he was the last to leave each afternoon in case anyone needed him to address any issues before the next day. His was always the last car in the parking lot.

Mr. Velarde dealt with personnel issues, student discipline, parent concerns, and district mandates. He had almost daily contact with law enforcement and community agencies to get ahead of any outside issues that might impact his school. During school, he walked the campus, visited classrooms, and met with district visitors, police officers, or social workers. He counseled students, parents, and staff. Late into the afternoon, he worked in his office returning calls and catching up on paperwork. Sound familiar?

No one would say that Mr. Velarde was not working his hardest on behalf of the school. People joked that he needed roller skates to meet the demands of his daily tasks! It was exhausting. Finally, after five years, the school had settled into a calm rhythm with no major emergencies on most days. Mr. Velarde was widely lauded as the person responsible for the improvement, and he himself felt the satisfaction of leading a school no longer in crisis. His was a "good" school. That is, until he learned about the school a few blocks away.

WHEN GREAT IS POSSIBLE, GOOD IS JUST NOT GOOD ENOUGH

One afternoon, the district held a principals' meeting at a neighboring school. The school was a stark exception for the neighborhood. It had quietly risen from the lowest rung of the achievement ladder to student achievement levels rivaling that of schools in the affluent areas of the city. To the group of principals, it seemed like the school was another challenged school just like theirs. Then one day they looked up and saw the school celebrated as a model, high-poverty, high-minority, high-performing school. The district asked Ms. Cortez, the principal of this successful school, to share the secret of her school's success with her colleagues. The principals were more than curious!

As Mr. Velarde drove the ten minutes to the school, he reflected on how much he and Ms. Cortez had in common. They had received assignments as principals the same year, and they had very similar student, community, and staff conditions. When they started, both their schools were listed among the lowest-achieving schools in the city. More than that, both principals had grown up in the neighborhood where they now served as principals, and the two had been classmates. Both principals had reputations for being hardworking, passionate, and committed to their schools and their community.

Yet their schools were now very different. Despite Mr. Velarde's accomplishments, his sincerest efforts had not translated into increased academic success for his students. In fact, he reasoned that student achievement was not yet his priority because there were so many more basic issues—such as safety, facilities, and basic relationship needs—to address. Thinking back, Mr. Velarde had an uncomfortable distant memory of his second year, when he had planned to address achievement but really did not know how to proceed. Somehow his time had become filled past the brim with other priorities.

NATURE OR NURTURE?

Educational equity is the measure of fairness in a school or district system. An assessment of equity answers the following question: Do all students, regardless of ZIP code, have access to and the appropriate support they need to succeed in the premium education that only some current experience? Must leaders be born to identify and eliminate inequitable systems and practices, or can leaders grow into equity leaders? Actually, both are true.

Some educators have instincts that make them quick to identify and disrupt educational injustices when they arise. For other educators, inequities remain largely invisible or ignored. For these leaders to become equity leaders, mentors must explicitly identify inequities and engage in reflective discussion to help them develop equity vision, mind-set, and disposition.

However, whether leaders have the instinct or develop an equity disposition over time, equity leaders must have the *will* to disrupt the status quo. Our experience has taught us that regardless of how they get there, all equity leaders are driven by one moral imperative, their True North, which propels them to action.

- Equity leadership begins with the unwavering conviction that every student is entitled to the premium schooling currently experienced by only some.
- Equity leaders flatly reject a fundamental concept that has ubiquitously seeped into the school systems and society as a whole without much challenge—the idea that some student groups are smarter and will naturally succeed, while others aren't and won't.
- Above all else, the single most significant barrier to success for students with a legacy of poor academic success is the educational glass ceiling—adult and institutional belief systems that hold different expectations for various student groups (Johnson & Avelar La Salle, 2010).

This chapter illustrates that the conviction of equity leaders to adamantly reject this notion is the catapult for turning around long-standing, historic patterns of underachievement for groups of students. The examples of Mr. Velarde and Ms. Cortez serve to highlight several concepts that are fundamental to the success of equity leaders as they take on systemic challenges to educational equity.

The Inevitability Assumption

A largely unspoken, extremely harmful, but undeniably widespread belief is that some students will do better than others expressly because of the group they represent. The *Inevitability Assumption* is the notion that schools simply are not capable of impacting negative patterns of achievement for some groups of students. There exists a belief that some students will prosper and others will struggle. This is attributed to the mistaken belief that demographics determine destiny.

The most insipid manifestation of this belief in practice is that students of color (especially African American, Latino, and Native American), poor students, students with learning disabilities, and other vulnerable students (i.e., those in foster care, transitional living situations, alternative educational settings, and the juvenile justice system, as well as English learners and unaccompanied minors) are simply not expected to be as successful in school as their peer groups who are in more privileged circumstances.

Equity Disposition

A clear marker of equity leaders is that they categorically reject the Inevitability Assumption. This behavior by those leaders demonstrates what it means to have an equity disposition. When the Inevitability Assumption goes unchallenged, it triggers decisions that at best perpetuate and exacerbate historic patterns of underachievement for entire groups of students.

Yet beliefs are personal, often private, internal worldviews. Unless others communicate their views, they are difficult to know. Does it matter what people believe about groups of people as long as they keep them quiet? Absolutely it matters! Here is why.

- Beliefs manifest themselves in decisions and actions.

  - Decisions and policy actions drive school systems.

    - Therefore, beliefs we hold about students drive institutional decisions and policy actions or inactions that directly impact students in our charge.

The Normalization of Failure

When the lack of success of an individual or group of students is so commonly accepted that it no longer causes us to pause or raises issues of any sort, failure has been normalized (Noguera & Wing, 2006). It becomes like the graffiti on the wall that has been there so long that it is no longer noticed by anyone walking past, which is exactly how things seep into culture.

The normalization of failure is a phenomenon that is the extremely dangerous on-the-ground by-product of the inevitability assumption and takes several forms. Sometimes it sounds like:

- The situation is terrible, but you should have seen it before!
- I wish it were better, but it could be way worse.
- That's just the way it is here.

Each of these is a variation on the same theme. Schools and districts that serve our most vulnerable students are at risk of normalizing failure in many ways that negatively impact students' achievement in school and beyond. Here are a few nonacademic examples that may be less obvious. When considering each one, ask: Would this be accepted in another area that serves students perceived as more privileged?

- Neglected facilities, dirty campuses, and/or broken furniture
- Tattered textbooks, limited teacher supplies, and/or insufficient or non-working technology
- Unfilled teacher positions covered by a series of daily or short-assignment substitutes
- High teacher or administrator turnover
- High student and staff absentee rates
- Disrespectful communication or limited relationship building between school personnel and students and/or parents
- Lack of professionalism on the part of school personnel regarding classroom or workspace orderliness, dress and grooming, and/or body language
- Acceptance of a lack of appropriateness of student dress, behavior, and/or language
- Lack of communication with parents regarding their children's successes or challenges at school
- Low expectations about parent and community behaviors or interactions on campus

NO ONE IS IMMUNE

While considering Ms. Cortez's school's impressive achievement gains, Mr. Velarde tuned into how tired and inept he felt. He felt disappointed in himself. How was it that student achievement never became a focus for him? He became even more introspective as he walked from Ms. Cortez's school parking lot past the front of the building. The walls were almost completely wrapped in banners acknowledging academic achievement from state and federal educational agencies as well as business and community organizations.

The banners were a public symbol of how the school was preparing students to be college bound. They became a source of extreme pride for children, parents, and the surrounding community. His head filled with questions as he arrived at the front entrance. As he walked under the entrance archway that students walked under each day, he looked up to see a bold motto that was prominently visible, proclaiming, "The door to college opens here."

Mr. Velarde passed through the entrance to the meeting room and sat quietly to hear about Ms. Cortez's secret to success. She stood before her colleagues, glanced at her notes for a second, and then turned the paper over. "I've thought long and hard about what to say to you," she said. "What accounts for the strides our school has made? Let me try to share some things I've learned that may help you."

Ms. Cortez's school was very complex, busy, crowded, and tense. She remembered that the thought in her mind when she opened her office door early each morning was, "I just hope nothing blows up today!" A good day was a quiet day. In fact, she felt like she turned the corner the first day she could work in her office and received no emergency call on her radio. "Whew! Today was a good day!"

Figure 1.1.   Photo of Ms. Cortez's School Entrance

Figure 1.2. Photo of Ms. Cortez's School Awards

Mr. Velarde listened intently, seeing himself in that description and anticipating the dreaded "however" he expected would begin the next sentence. "However," she continued, "after several months, I began to identify some hard truths." She went on to say that she slowly realized that some students receive an excellent education at her school . . . but not all. Further, she admitted that many students were experiencing an excellent education some days, but not every day, and not every part of every day.

At some point, Ms. Cortez questioned whether she was participating in the "soft bigotry of low expectations" that often permeates schools like hers. *Gulp*. Might that explain the widespread satisfaction about her school's improved climate and the lack of concern about poor scholarship? Was this perhaps a normalization of failure?

How did she, who had attended these same schools when she was a child, not pick up on this right away? Was it possible that she had somehow internalized the Inevitability Assumption? Once Ms. Cortez was able to bring herself to fully articulate these thoughts in her own mind, she was overwhelmed by a dissatisfaction that would transform her leadership style from that day forward.

TROUBLE FINDER

Ms. Cortez explained that she struggled to accept the fact that on her watch, academic failure had been normalized. She told her colleagues that she was going to share with them her most valuable leadership lesson: "See yourself as someone who is personally responsible for giving every student the best education that exists anywhere, not the best education in your neighborhood."

This idea resonated with Mr. Velarde, but he wondered how he could put it into practice. How are equity leaders different from other committed leaders? What do equity leaders *do* that result in impactful outcomes, especially for our most vulnerable students with long legacies of poor success in school?

It is profound when we as leaders arrive at a place where we see educational justice as our mission. The next step is the most important, however: We must translate our will to promote equity into deliberate action. *Equity actions* include steps to change external structures and systems. As Ms. Cortez noted, they can also be internal actions that shape the dispositional characteristics of equity leaders themselves.

Reframing Your Leadership Mind-set

Ms. Cortez surprised the group when she explained that she did not attribute her school's success to what she *did* differently, though she did take many impactful actions. Altering her mind-set about her role as a leader was the most significant change.

Our mandate is to ensure that each student receives a high-quality education, without qualification. A common question among equity leaders is whether a school would be good enough for our own children to attend. This question is often posed when trying to inspire school and district improvement efforts. Ms. Cortez added more transformative power to the question by asking the principals the following:

- If the law required that the family members of anyone who works in a school must attend that school, would anything at the school be different?
- Would leaders see themselves and their mandate any differently?
- Would leaders spend their time differently?

The work of equity leaders is complex and taxing, but it is also invigorating and steeped in personal and professional satisfaction. The driving force that keeps spirits and energy high enough to meet equity challenges is that it is simply true, right, and just that every student has an equitable opportunity to acquire the benefits of a premium education. Educational justice for all is the conviction that inspires courageous action. [In other words, lead from your personal "why." Why are you driven to promoting educational equity?]

Assume Something Is Wrong, Then Try to Prove Yourself Wrong

Here is a powerful mind-set nuance that at first glance is confusing. Rather than being pleased by a day with no emergencies, assume that some students are not getting their due on any given day or time. Assume inequities exist. The laws of probability suggest that nothing is perfect all the time. This is a personal stance that creates an internal sense of urgency and attentiveness that can turn the tide of legacy systems that work against certain students.

Ms. Cortez shared that more than strategies, plans, activities, or interventions, the driving force behind the positive movement at her school was preceding external actions by defining her own equity disposition. This frame of mind colored everything she thought and did. Classroom visits, campus walk-throughs, staff meetings, professional learning sessions, feedback to staff—everything changed about how she spent her time once she became comfortable assuming something could be improved every day. She made it her mission to find those areas and address them.

The power of assuming inequities exist crystalizes the role of an equity educational leader in actionable terms. Set out each day to find out where opportunities are being missed. As one concrete practice, student shadowing is an example of how leaders can operationalize an equity disposition to support powerful teaching and learning for every student.

- During classroom visits, focus on how students receive instruction (considering more than the steps of the lesson).

    - Sit in a seat in the vicinity of a student who represents the profile of the type of student you want to learn more about, and experience learning as that student does. Make sure you can see the student's face.
    - Then sit in a seat near a student you believe to be less vulnerable and experience learning as that student does. Make sure you can see the student's face.

Is everyone receiving the same educational benefit? Is the lesson reaching some students more than others? Check for:

- who gets called on and how often;
- the nature of the interactions (instructive, procedural, or behavioral);
- if and how students volunteer responses;
- where students are seated relative to one another;
- what happens when students do not understand;

- the nature of the students' engagement; and
- the types of questions asked and answered.

In other words, seek out those opportunities to improve learning for all students, but especially those on the fringe, where schooling is often experienced differently. Adopting the equity mind-set propels leaders to zero in on areas of continuous improvement we might not otherwise notice.

Ms. Cortez described one heartbreaking situation at her school that typifies the importance of "looking for trouble." Discipline in her school had improved dramatically over the course of her first few years at the school. Suspensions were almost down to zero, and there were no expulsions. This was a much-celebrated accomplishment, given the school's long history of poor academic climate. By the end of her second year at the school, she had checked discipline off her worry list.

In her third year, Ms. Cortez got struck by the equity ache in her belly, sparked by her moral compass, and crystalized by her "looking for trouble" disposition. While walking the school, she noticed that although students were not being suspended or expelled, a number of students were seated in the back of classrooms, benched on the yard, or required to stay after school. Seen through equity eyes, she realized that systemic practices of student discipline had evolved that lacked formal documentation. It appeared that, although informal, these practices resulted in serious disciplinary and academic consequences for some students.

She found that given the district's push to reduce the number of suspensions and expulsions, staff members had devised a system of consequences for students who behaved in ways deemed inappropriate. This explained the principal's observations. Although excluding and isolating students is problematic, the more painful aspect was her suspicion that students representing particular groups might be disproportionately receiving more consequences than others.

Use Data to Describe Inequitable Systems

Seek and ye shall find. Looking for trouble in schools will unearth them. However, once you find a possible inequity, the most important step is to take action to disrupt the system that promotes that inequity. This seems obvious, but experience has taught us that simply knowing something is wrong does not necessarily lead to fixing it.

Needing to act, Ms. Cortez brought her concern about school discipline practices to her leadership team, which defended the system in a lengthy discussion. Once all issues were on the table, the principal explained that the practices were troubling her because student conduct actions needed to be documented to reveal patterns that would enable the team to help students improve over time.

Ms. Cortez was honest in sharing her worry about the possible disproportionate application of disciplinary practices for some student groups. She was keenly aware of the advantages of asking the team to join her in a quest to discover how the informal system was being applied.

Compelled by her true, right, and just concerns, the team came together and devised a documentation system that resulted in quarterly reports, by class, identifying which students (by demographic and achievement level) received consequences, who assigned the consequences, a description of the consequences, and any changes in behavior after those consequences. Table 1.1 displays a sample report template.

The team then developed the same documentation system for yard supervisors and other staff. After a few months, the leadership team reviewed the reports with the principal and discovered several disturbing patterns.

- Only 20 percent of the student body was African American, but 75 percent of all disciplinary consequences were assigned to African American students, almost all boys.
- Ninety-five percent of the disciplinary consequences were issued to nine students, each repeated many times, some with as many as fifteen consequences in two months.
- Five adults on campus—out of thirty-five teachers, four yard supervisors, and an assistant principal—issued 90 percent of all consequences.
- Of the nine most frequently punished students:

  - Three students received consequences from multiple adults. These students struggled with behavior in many settings.
  - Six students received consequences from only one adult, as many as seventeen times each. In other words, each student was punished only when interacting with one particular adult.

Table 1.1.   Informal Discipline Log

Student	Ethnicity	Gender	Referred by	Offense	Consequence	Behavior after Consequence

• The students with the most disciplinary consequences were among the lowest-achieving students in the school, performing lower that year than in years prior.

Build Collective Equity Muscle

These findings point to the sobering fact that as microcosms of larger society, schools and districts are as at risk as any other institution of systemic bias. Once found, these systems cannot stand, and equity leaders must take action to disrupt them. Ms. Cortez freely shared the information with the entire staff, facilitated tough conversations in large and small groups, and had private talks with individuals. She made it clear to all that the story told by the data was not acceptable and that systems must change.

The leadership team reviewed the discipline reports every month. After each data review, the team members determined what actions they would take and test to see if outcomes would improve. After about three years at the school, Ms. Cortez felt confident enough in her "looking for trouble" stance that she shared it with her staff, challenging them to adopt their own equity disposition.

Ms. Cortez shared with her colleagues that she had to explain the difference between "looking for trouble" and "causing trouble" to a few of her folks! Overall, though, the school community embraced this Equity Hook as a reminder of what it means to be an equity leader.

Ms. Cortez's reflections left Mr. Velarde to contemplate the health of his own equity heart and the clarity of his moral imperative. This is exactly how leaders grow as equity leaders. Even those who are confident, natural-born equity leaders must regularly take a step back from life and consider what drives the work they do. Are you clear about what drives you in your work? Do your daily actions as a leader always align? What are you doing to challenge the normalization of failure on behalf of your most vulnerable students?

EQUITY HOOK: GO TO WORK AND LOOK FOR TROUBLE

SUMMARY

This chapter narrates a story about the leaders of two challenged urban schools that struggled with a long history of low achievement. We met two principals in different stages of their development as equity leaders, one growing intuitively and the other through deliberate self-reflection.

This tale of two schools corresponds directly to a tale of two principals, both of whom had the vision and initiative to lead a school, but only one of whom had an equity muscle that produced a school culture for successful outcomes for all students. The examples of Mr. Velarde and Ms. Cortez demonstrate how easy it is for failure to be normalized for some groups of students, and how susceptible we all are to falling into that abyss.

This chapter also describes other, less obvious ways that practices, behaviors, and basic academic standards are often compromised in educational settings in ways that impact our most vulnerable students. Observing school practices with equity vision propelled one principal to confront and address the inequities. She used her equity disposition to "look for trouble" and take equity action to address inequities.

We have argued that some equity leaders function from an instinctive nature. Others come to see the light of equity through reflection, new evidence, and the interruption of traditional policies and practices. The path to equity leadership may be different, but our Equity True North makes the power of equity leadership profound.

Changing long-standing patterns of underachievement for certain groups of students is not simple, but it is absolutely possible. It requires leaders who make educational equity their moral compass (Fullan, 2011) and build collective equity muscle from three foundational tenets:

1. Every school system is perfectly designed to get the results it currently gets.
2. Every student deserves the premium education that only some currently experience.
3. Every educator has a moral obligation to help our most vulnerable students receive the best education available anywhere.

EQUITY CONCEPTS

- *The Inevitability Assumption:* This is the notion that, by virtue of conditions outside of the control of schooling, some students will prosper and others will struggle. It is the mistaken belief that demographics determine destiny.
- *The Normalization of Failure:* When the lack of success of an individual or group of students is so common that it no longer causes pause of any sort, failure has been normalized in the culture of an institution.
- *Equity Disposition:* Equity leaders adopt this stance that every part of every day is an opportunity to seek out inequities and to disrupt systems that limit success for groups of students.
- *Equity Muscle:* This is the courage and adeptness to address inequities, which strengthen each time a leader works through an equity issue.

- *Collective Equity Muscle:* This is the powerful phenomenon that occurs when groups of people share a moral imperative and create a community equity leader identity.

EQUITY ACTIONS

- Reframe your mind-set. Engage in deep self-reflection about what drives you to action as an educational leader. Consider adopting the conviction that it is true, right, and just that every student receive the premium education currently experienced by only some.
- Assume inequities exist, then try to prove yourself wrong. Take the stance that inequitable practices occur regularly, whether they come to you as a problem or not. On a daily basis, intentionally form hunches about possible inequities in your school or district and follow up on them to see if they lead to an area that can be improved to support better student outcomes.
- Use data to disrupt inequitable systems. Remember that every system is perfectly designed to get the results it is currently getting. Describe inequitable practices using data (quantitative and/or qualitative) and focus on changing the deep systemic structures that underpin inequities to engender long-term, sustainable improved outcomes for all students, especially our most vulnerable.

Chapter Two

Data as an Equity Engine

Equity Hook: Beware the Wallpaper Effect!

Have you ever wondered . . .

- How comfortable do you or others feel when people discuss data?
- Whether you have the expertise to use data as an equity tool?
- Why reports don't always match what you perceive to be true in your school or district?
- If you could learn to use data to accelerate student success?
- What can change for students' lives when we use data to uncover deeply rooted systemic inequities in school systems?

Wallpaper is decorating magic! With little effort or cost, it can transform a room from a dingy space into a bright new area anyone would love and enjoy. However, as our equity leader in this chapter discovered, wallpaper can be deceiving. It can mask many imperfections below the surface. Some imperfections might be small; others might be deep and structural, putting in jeopardy the very foundation of the home. This chapter will describe how this threat makes it imperative that equity leaders remember to beware the Wallpaper Effect!

Laura was the superintendent of an award-winning K–12 school district. Education agencies, community organizations, and even a national foundation honored her school district for being diverse, low income, and also high achieving. Students achieved at much higher levels than those in similar districts in the county and state, outperforming them on achievement, graduation rates, and college eligibility rates. They also had better outcomes than other districts in terms of dropout rates and student discipline patterns for English learners. The board, staff, parents, and community were extremely proud of their district. Flags and banners publicizing their achievements hung at every school in the district. By all accounts, this was a wonderful district for staff and students.

The district had always been strong academically, yet Laura had developed a personal disquiet about something for a few years. While the district achievement profile had been impressive a long time, she knew that not all student groups were doing equally well, and that just did not sit well with her.

The Latino and African American students (60 percent of the student body combined) in her district were not having the same success as their Asian and White counterparts (40 percent of the student body). Laura encouraged key people in the district to think about and take action to support schools to close the achievement gap between Latino and African American students compared with Asian and White students. It worked.

On state exam results for language arts and mathematics, the gap between the higher-performing students and the others was reduced by more than half in five years. This remarkable improvement was noticed in the county and by the media, winning the district even more praise.

On one of her regular site visits, Laura decided to focus exclusively on the high schools, where she observed and felt high energy and vitality from staff and students. She walked through classrooms and saw engaged students and skilled teachers. Counselors were in their offices speaking to students and also in classrooms presenting information about graduation and college. Administrators were walking their campuses engaging with students and staff, and meeting with parents in their offices.

The positive culture of the schools was palpable and indicated to the superintendent that the district emphasis on powerful teaching, learning, and leading was having an important impact. Yet in the car on the ride back to her office, she felt a dull ache in the pit of her stomach.

WHAT'S THE MATTER, LAURA?

Equity work is complex and requires 360 degree attention to outcomes. In truth, the parts that make up educational systems are so interrelated that addressing one issue almost always affects another. This domino effect can be positive but can also result in unintended consequences that are negative for some students—or even for the adults serving students. The sobering fact is that we educators are often so busy doing the work that we do not stop to reflect on and evaluate potential unintended consequences of our well-intentioned efforts.

Guarding against unintended consequences requires vigilant use of data—all types of data. Using data is central to our impact as equity leaders because it reveals whether or not our efforts are producing the intended outcomes. If not, data can reveal areas of need where we can make timely adjustments and get back on course.

Here is the rub: It used to be that data were difficult to get in school systems. Only those considered "data experts" really had a handle on available information. Over time, however, data have become much more accessible. In fact, in many respects, school systems are now data-drenched! Offices are crowded with notebooks filled with data reports disaggregated every which way the software produces it. Software programs cut data in more ways than any human could ever or would ever want to consume.

The existence of data is no longer rare. However, skilled use of data to promote educational equity *is* rare.

- Must we all become statisticians to be effective equity leaders?
- Must we become programmers to create specialized reports?

Not at all. However, we must develop equity vision so that we become critical consumers of the data that are accessible.

Here is why: Inequitable systems and practices are just like sand crabs on a beach. They burrow below the surface and become invisible to most people, covered up by many things. In the example of sand crabs, they are hidden by sand, shells, kelp, or sea glass. Likewise, educational inequities are often situated inside school and district structures covered by the daily rituals of education. In both cases—sand crabs and educational inequities—whether we are aware of them or not, they will show themselves eventually and may even pinch!

As equity leaders, we should ask ourselves, might available data be:

- masking underlying inequities that could perpetuate historical under-achievement?
- obscuring the educational glass ceiling that is creating a barrier for some students and not others?

The Wallpaper Effect

One of the most common barriers to promoting equitable educational systems for students is the inability of equity leaders to skillfully mitigate the Wallpaper Effect, in which decisions are made based on superficial data that actually cover up real, deeply rooted inequities (Johnson & Avelar La Salle, 2010). Data stories must drive our equity actions. If the data story is accurate and complete, as we will demonstrate in this chapter, we are able to employ equity actions that have the potential to transform student lives in positive ways. However, if our data story is wrong or incomplete, our actions can actually do harm to students. Therefore, a major challenge to equity leaders is developing the systems to identify, collect, disaggregate, and analyze data in a way that that alerts them to the Wallpaper Effect.

Data Inquiry with an Equity Lens

The use of aggregate or single-indicator data makes us especially susceptible to the Wallpaper Effect. In the example of Laura's district, aggregate data showed that the gap between the groups had closed significantly. As a result, most people in the district believed that their equity issue had been resolved. Even though the gap was reduced, the achievement of Asian and White students remained significantly higher than that of Latino and African American students; however, only the percentage gap reduction and district averages were the figures that received public notice. Unchecked by a truly in-depth application of data inquiry with an equity lens, the Wallpaper Effect resulted in widespread belief that the district was high performing. No attention was paid to the differential achievement between student groups that existed for decades.

Combination Data

Combining two or more indicators is a powerful data strategy for peeling back the wallpaper. Combination data are information sets that we overlap to help us more closely understand the complexities related to equity questions. Using combination data helps peel back layers to expose conditions hidden below the surface.

For example, Laura's district was a highly diverse, high-poverty district. Data demonstrated that the average achievement of minority students was impressive, as was the achievement of high-poverty students and English learners. As Laura grew as an equity leader, she began to ask deeper questions that could be answered only through the use of combination data, which led to even more questions. As she engaged in the data this way, she helped the district break through the Wallpaper Effect to reveal and understand a much more complex story.

Laura studied the standard data reports for demographic outcomes. This is what she found:

- The district is diverse, as defined by 80 percent of the students being minorities (Latino, African American, Asian), and their achievement as a group is strong.
- The district serves primarily low-income students, and that group achieves well.
- Unlike most other districts in the county, the district's large English learner population achieved at high levels.

The use of combination data enables us to gain clarity and precision in our understanding so that strategic equity actions can target and support accelerated improvements in student success. In this district, as in most, many complexities and nuances existed that needed uncovering. Laura and the team needed to continue to peel back the data. Table 2.1 compares what was learned about student groups.

In schools and districts with complex demographic profiles, there is a high risk of inaccurately identifying inequitable outcomes for students. When using only a single indicator, interpretations of what the data are showing are often inadequate and not robust enough for sound decision making. Not all economically disadvantaged students are the same, nor are all English learners, all Latino students, all African American students, or any other group, for that matter. No group of students is monolithic, regardless of label.

WHAT'S BEHIND THAT WALLPAPER?

Here is the more accurate story told once Laura became skilled in the use of combination data with an equity lens. In this district, Asian students were the highest-performing group, and their labels as low income and English learners made the numbers for vulnerable students look very high, giving the impression that they were very successful. No equity issues here!

Combining data points, however, indicated the following unexpected findings and led to more questions and a sense of urgency about badly needed equity actions:

- The highest-performing students were Asian, regardless of economic status or English proficiency level. This finding led to the following next-level questions:

  - Why is lower English proficiency not the barrier to achievement for Asian students the way it is for others?
  - Why do low-income Asian students do better than other low-income students?

- The lowest-achieving students were Latinos, who were also low-income students and who were labeled English learners mostly since kindergarten. This led to the following question:

  - Why were Latino students not succeeding after so long in school?

- Though not a large number, Latino students who began as English learners but were reclassified to English fluent during elementary school achieved at significantly higher rates than other English learners, scoring just below

Table 2.1.   Comparison of Relevant Student Profiles by Race and Ethnicity

	Latino	*Asian*	*African American*	*White*
History in US Schools	• Mostly US born • Most started kindergarten in US	Mostly immigrated during school years having attended school in their home country	US born	US born
Income Levels	Mostly low income	Mostly low income	Mixed income	Mixed income
English Proficiency	• Labeled English learners • Mostly English speakers, but not reclassified because of low academic levels	Originally labeled English learners but reclassified to English fluent by high school (met academic criteria)	Native English speakers	Native English speakers
Parent Profiles	• New immigrant or first generation • Varying education levels • In US for economic opportunity	• Mostly refugees • Many with higher education levels in home country (but working labor jobs in US) • In US to flee political turmoil in home countries	Mixed educational levels	Mixed educational levels

the average of Asian students. This was true regardless of their income or English proficiency status, which led to the following question:

• Why were these particular Latino students, who began like most other Latino students, so much more successful?

- White student achievement was split, with students in better economic conditions performing better than low-income students. This led to the following question:

  - Why did economic status play such a significant role for these students, but not for all others equally?

- For African American students, economic status did not play a significant role in achievement. Students with higher or lower economic status tended to perform at the lower end of the school average, which led to the following questions:

  - Why did economic status play such a negligible role in their achievement?
  - Why was achievement for higher-income African Americans not stronger than for lower-income African Americans?

The story told by combination data caused Laura to worry that the district was enjoying an undeserved reputation largely anchored in the Wallpaper Effect that showed overall high achievement averages. This phenomenon resulted in a district-wide complacency regarding lower success by some student groups. This did not match Laura's sense of urgency. Laura's identity as an equity leader was growing through this process.

Other Data

Laura needed to continue her data quest by using "other data." Other data include: (a) data not typically analyzed or (b) typical data viewed through an equity lens. Often, we analyze standardized test or other indicator averages as a starting point. We are not of the mind that such information is irrelevant or to be dismissed. It definitely tells a story—that is, the beginning of a story. The equity approach is to:

1. move from using only aggregate data and expand to include disaggregated data;
2. use combination data sets; and
3. ultimately include other data to arrive at deeper understandings. These other data can uncover insightful information about the academic culture of a school and how students are faring in the system. These data give clues to what needs to change in the culture and practices of schools and districts (Avelar La Salle & Johnson, 2016; Johnson, 2002; Johnson & Avelar La Salle 2010; Lindsey, Graham, Westphal, & Jew, 2008; McKinsey & Company, 2009; Noguera & Wing, 2006).

Laura acknowledged that all students were improving on state exams, which she believed measured important academic competencies. The state accountability system was predicated on these results, as were the state, federal, and foundation awards the district received. The parents and community valued those results. They were important.

Yet there are other, less visible data that are neither as widely shared nor part of formal accountability measures but are nonetheless critical pieces of the equity story. These powerful data influence outcomes, have long-term consequences for students, and are critical elements related to issues of equity and social justice. Other data have the potential to spotlight institutional behaviors and often paint a very different picture about true conditions that are incongruent with what we say we believe or want for students.

As Laura developed her equity muscle, this was a big part of what troubled her. She was now well aware that the positive attention enjoyed by the district was largely because of district averages on state exams. While these numbers were important to her, other outcomes that she believed were transformational received far less attention.

WHAT OUTCOMES WAS LAURA CONCERNED ABOUT?

Laura was particularly uneasy about one key indicator that she considered a life-changer: the low numbers of Latino and African American students who enrolled in four-year universities. Laura knew that many Latino and African American students faced economic and linguistic challenges—but she also knew that the Asian students, mostly children of refugees, faced similar economic and linguistic challenges, yet they were faring much better with college enrollment.

Something deep inside Laura refused to accept the explanation that was silently practiced in her district—that lesser outcomes were inevitable for some groups of students. Were these patterns inevitable, or could the district do more to promote improved outcomes for all of its students?

Laura realized that she needed to take a step back and intentionally reflect on the story told through her data inquiry process. In doing so she admitted to herself that she did not know how to lead her district past its current state toward achieving educational equity for all students. After considering this fact, she spoke to her cabinet about her desire to get help.

Collaborate with an Equity Partner

Many educators feel strongly about issues of equity and educational justice. However, not all educators with an equity heart have the background and experience to know how to address systemic inequities. Ask for help. Even those of us who identify as equity leaders are always working to strengthen our equity muscle and must admit that we do not know how to deal with every situation.

Having an equity heart is just not enough to change deeply rooted educational systems. Laura turned to a trusted friend who was a fellow equity leader but—more than that—also an equity strategist. Laura's friend had experience addressing challenges posed by inequitable educational systems, so Laura invited her to serve as her equity adviser. This partnership led the district to implement several strategic equity actions that set the district on a course it might not otherwise have taken.

Conduct an Equity Discovery Study

This action requires that you take in-depth, honest stock of your condition. Organize the discovery around the following questions:

- What is the achievement profile? Use combination data to describe the achievement story, layer by layer. In Laura's district, the high-level story was that the district was doing well, but data analyzed through an equity lens uncovered something different.

  - Not all students in poverty were struggling equally, and not all English learners were struggling equally either.
  - Combining data indicators of income levels, ethnicity, and language proficiency led to some sensitive questions. Why were Asian students doing better than Latino students, both of whom had large numbers of English learners and low-income students?

- What best explains the achievement profile? Use other data and combination indicators to understand why achievement profiles are as they are for different students.
- What can be done to accelerate improvements in achievement profiles for students that concern us? Resist the temptation to believe that everything has been tried, and do not become discouraged by factors over which you have little control. If that occurs, reframe the question and ask:

  - If conditions at the school were such that all students were successful, what would those conditions be?

To engage in an Equity Discovery Study, Laura's equity thought-partner suggested the district establish a study team composed of district and school administrators, teacher leaders, and counselors. The team focused on examining data for the district's five high schools, reasoning that achievement disparities at this level can have the most life-changing consequences and reflect the entire K–12 system. The exploration began with a review of all available data.

When the team members looked at their reports, they were proud of the overall long-term, sustained improvements across the district marked by increased proficiency levels, English language mastery, graduation rates, and college eligibility. The study team wondered, "What is Laura worried about?"

Peel Back the Wallpaper

Be suspicious of summary data. Become accustomed to the following inquiry protocol displayed in figure 2.1 that peels back the layers of data to get to the systemic equity jams.

Laura's equity thought-partner suspected the district was experiencing the Wallpaper Effect, so the next step was for the team to peel back layers of that wallpaper. The team conducted focus groups and interviewed a variety of people whose voices could contribute to deeper understanding, including:

- students from each demographic group;
- students who did and did not complete their university prerequisite sequence;
- all teachers of advanced, regular, and remedial courses;
- counselors; and

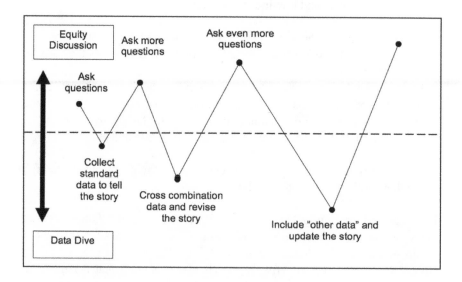

Figure 2.1.   Protocol for Peeling Back the Wallpaper.

- district and school administrators.

The team asked initial questions that led to second- and third-level questions. Team members were fascinated as they peeled back the layers and began to gain clarity on the impact of the district's past and present practices.

What Does Student Government Have to Do with This?

In one compelling example, the team decided to study the profile of the most successful students in district schools, including students from every ethnicity, race, language proficiency category, and economic group. Rather than focusing on struggling students, team members wanted to learn what the schools were doing well by looking at students who were succeeding.

They had a sense that students who were most involved in school were most successful—and the data confirmed this. Students who participated in student government, for instance, were among the highest achieving at every high school. The team members knew that White and Asian students held most student government posts. The question was, why?

Here are four theories posited by various groups at the school:

1. Latino and African American students were simply not as interested in participating in student government because they favored sports or needed to have after-school jobs.
2. The grade requirements to run for office explained the lack of equal participation, imagining that many Latino and African American students were probably disqualified from running because of poor grades.
3. Cultural norms influenced Latino and African American students; these students, they guessed, probably preferred to spend their free time with students of their own ethnicity and culture.
4. Asian and White students might harbor biases against Latino and African American students and may have intentionally avoided interacting with them.

But the focus group data—especially the student voices—suggested a completely different explanation that no one on the team could have ever imagined.

WHOOMP! THERE IT IS!

At each high school, students were encouraged to run for office at a lunchtime recruitment fair held during the final month of school. Existing student government officers were at a booth to entice students to get information and to recruit them to run. Most often, students visited the booth because they were friends with one of the officers standing there. And students often make friends by being in the same classes.

Why Are Students in Advanced Placement Classes Mostly Asian?

Based on these interviews, the study team members now suspected that differences in student government participation were related more to class placement practices as well as legacy issues of race or culture. They followed this new hunch by peeling back the layers further, gathering other data, including:

- counselor-student contact rosters;
- schedules of counselor visits by class level;
- written course placement criteria compared with student transcripts;
- demographic distribution of classes by level; and
- school maps showing the location of advanced classes and other classes in relation to college information, student bulletins, and counseling activities.

Adding these other data into the mix resulted in some sobering and disturbing findings. Most revealing was that some policies and practices the schools had assumed were good and fair were actually stifling many students' academic achievement.

Placement Patterns

Placement in advanced classes was not proportional to the makeup of the student body. Eighty-five percent of students in advanced classes were Asian or White, though they represented only 30 percent of the student population. Lower-level classes were primarily populated with Latino and African American students. After analyzing these data, the team members asked, "Why does this pattern exist?" This is what they found:

- Asian and White students who met placement criteria—which included grades and test scores—for advanced classes were automatically assigned to those classes. In addition, some Asian and White students who did *not* meet the strict placement criteria were regularly enrolled in advanced classes through a backdoor process that included parent, student, or teacher request. These findings expose that informal practices exist in the schools' cultures that advocate for and favor some student groups who get access to information on how to navigate course placements.
- In contrast, only half the Latino and African American students who were qualified for automatic placement were assigned to advanced classes. These qualified students were not assigned to advanced classes if adults

did not recommend them or if the students opted out. The Latino and African American students who were interviewed by the study team reported that sometimes teachers, administrators, or parents did not believe they had the necessary "study habits" to be successful.
- Further, qualified students who opted out of the advanced classes shared that they felt uneasy about taking those courses for two major reasons:

  - Teachers had not encouraged them to take advanced courses, but rather had warned them about the difficulty of these courses, which made the students fear that they would fail.
  - The students worried that they would feel isolated because so few of their friends were in those classes. In general, Latino and African American students got the sense that those courses were not really meant for them—that they did not belong there. Regrettably, this was a common occurrence in all the high schools.

The study team also wanted to find out more about the few Latino and African American students who *were* placed in advanced classes. The team examined the data and found that these students were most often in the Advancement Via Individual Determination (AVID) program. AVID is a research-tested program with a long, successful track record of supporting underrepresented students through a college-going academic path. AVID students are assigned a rigorous course schedule, receive focused academic attention, and have strong advocacy from their AVID counselor and teachers.

The bottom line was that school and district practices and expectations for different groups had more to do with the differential placement of students than anyone realized. It became crystal clear to the team how and why inequitable patterns in students graduating university-ready continued to be perpetuated. Now that the study team was keenly aware of the inequities in the system, the district needed to shift, revise, and eliminate many of its current practices that were causing poor outcomes for some groups of students. For example:

- It was evident that the AVID program was successful and that the program needed to expand to include more historically underrepresented students.
- The district needed to recruit students for college preparatory courses in ways that would ensure that all students had peers in the programs to prevent students from feeling isolated.
- The district needed a process for student placement that was not predicated on perceptions of student work ethic by students, and needed to equally inform all student groups and their parents about placement opportunities and the live consequences of each option.

Under Laura's leadership, the study team designed a plan that would address these unconscious biases that were part of the district's system (Fiarman, 2016). As a first step, Laura and the study team shared their findings with the entire staff, and together they designed an equity plan that included using combination data and other data to measure equitable outcomes and district practices related to equity.

College Counseling

The study team believed that counseling played a pivotal role in providing students with college-going guidance, so team members interviewed counselors to see whether they had information that would help explain the different outcomes by student group. Counselors reported that they gave information frequently and equally to all students. Some counselors shared their perception that certain student groups were just naturally more interested than others in going to college.

The team asked counselors to peel back another layer and to review their counseling logs to check for anything that might help explain the outcome gaps. This inquiry led to findings that surprised even the counselors! The logs indicated that counselors were correct in reporting that they visited classes to provide information about university preparation with great frequency—advanced classes, that is.

Counselors visited lower-level English classes once each year and provided information only about high school graduation. This was not a formal, written policy of exclusion, but rather an informal practice that had evolved over time on the basis of unexamined and inaccurate perceptions about what different groups of students needed and were capable of achieving.

Another revealing finding related to the way the schools shared written communication about college attendance. The adults believed that placing college information on the main public bulletin board provided equal access to all students. They assumed that Asian and White students took more interest than Latino and African American students in reading the posted weekly notices.

However, a walk to that bulletin board helped the team see that the location of lower-level classes within the school made it highly unlikely that those students would ever be in its vicinity. The board was located right outside the Advanced Placement (AP) classrooms and near the honors classrooms, providing an excellent information source conveniently accessible only to advanced students. As a result of these findings, the team took the following equity actions:

- As part of the equity plan, the team decided that every student should receive the same college-going information and that written information should be shared through multiple avenues.
- Information would be placed in locations that were accessible to all students, and counselors would adjust their time to focus on students needing more support.
- The school team would overcommunicate the college-going messages to students who previously were not considered college going. This required changes in assumptions and expectations for counselors, teachers, administrators, and students alike.
- The team established data systems to continuously analyze, monitor, and make recommendations to sustain equitable district practices designed to provide all students with equitable access and opportunity for success in college preparatory classes.

WHAT MAKES LAURA AN EQUITY LEADER? YOU DECIDE!

Opening herself and her district to collaboration with an equity thought-partner, Laura and her team learned to peel back the layers of data and discovered that although economic and social conditions were undeniable, these conditions did not entirely explain outcomes. Systemic policies and practices—both formal and informal—were at the root of the inequities, which perpetuated and exacerbated gaps. These structures and systems had become normalized.

Analyzing data through an equity lens, Laura and the team uncovered many false assumptions about the reasons for the achievement gaps between the different groups. Peeling back the wallpaper produced clarity about some policies and practices that the district needed to change as well as other policies and practices it needed to institutionalize so that all students would have equitable outcomes. The study team members felt empowered because they were able to uncover data the district could use to guide it to higher outcomes for all students.

By exposing the Wallpaper Effect, Laura led her district to make changes to key policies and practices that resulted in truly impressive gains for *all* students. The district again earned public acknowledgment—this time, for achieving remarkable outcomes for historically less successful Latino and African American students, sending more of these students to four-year universities than any other district in the state. Laura was proud that the systemic changes they made resulted in more life-changing options for students.

EQUITY HOOK: BEWARE THE WALLPAPER EFFECT!

SUMMARY

In this chapter we have described the Wallpaper Effect. The example demonstrates how the Wallpaper Effect worked in a school district to adversely affect groups of students. Students got lost in data that told erroneous stories about student success. The superintendent grew into a powerful equity leader advocating for all her students because she learned to use data as a tool to uncover hidden inequitable practices. This chapter describes her equity journey and the stages of growth that she and her staff experienced.

The chapter describes how Laura and her study team, with the assistance of an equity adviser, uncovered other data that helped them discover how their systemic practices were inhibiting opportunities for some groups of students. This involved developing their data fluency so they could peel back layers of data in ways that had never previously been done. As a result, the district was transformed by its modification of policies and practices.

Districts that are committed to equity for all students must be aware of the Wallpaper Effect and take the necessary steps to learn how to appropriately peel back the layers of data to uncover and eliminate hidden inequities. As equity leaders, we must be on alert for the Wallpaper Effect and its powerful negative impact on decisions made about students.

Our equity leader, Laura, illustrates how equitable outcomes are possible and achievable when we have the will to pursue equity and the courage and skill to use data as an equity tool to challenge inequitable systems that harm students.

EQUITY CONCEPTS

- *The Wallpaper Effect:* The Wallpaper Effect is a term associated with the use of superficial data that cover up real, deeply rooted inequities, which is a constant risk when addressing systemic inequities.
- *Combination Data:* Combination data are data points that overlap to reveal more closely the complexities related to equity questions. Using combination data helps us peel back layers to expose conditions previously hidden below the surface.
- *Data Inquiry with an Equity Lens:* Data fluency in this context is the act of interacting with data to counteract the ever-present risk of the Wallpaper Effect.
- *Other Data:* These include (a) data not typically analyzed and (b) typical data viewed through an equity lens.

EQUITY ACTIONS

- Collaborate with an equity partner. Open yourself up to a trusted third-party person or team to help you ask the critical questions that you may not be able to see because you are too close to a situation.
- Conduct an Equity Discovery Study. Engage in a systematic process of analyzing other data and combination data to test hunches and arrive at better questions to help achieve a deep understanding of systemic inequities.
- Peel back the wallpaper. Make the invisible visible by analyzing data, layer by layer, to get at the root of hidden systemic inequities.

Part II

How Do Impactful Equity Leaders Lead?

Chapter Three

When Adult Behavior Poses Equity Challenges

Equity Hook: Everyone's Got a Story

Have you ever wondered . . .

- Why adults sometimes behave badly?
- How to respond when adults are difficult to interact with?
- What to do when you feel disrespected by other adults while leading for equity?
- How to be an effective equity leader when adults are disruptive?

Every equity leader will encounter adults whose behavior is baffling. Equity issues bring out the best and the worst in people because they lean on people's very personal belief systems. An interesting note is that two people involved in the same equity discussion will often react completely differently! Why is that, and how can equity leaders effectively work with *all* people? Remembering that "everyone's got a story" is a comforting as well as very practical Equity Hook in these situations, as the equity leader in this chapter discovered.

Dahlia was a young, committed school district administrator who, in an effort to impact as many educational leaders as possible, also taught leadership courses for the county office of education. Her energy seemed boundless and her experience teaching in a high-poverty school fueled her desire to help make education more equitable for all students.

Her students were new school administrators from around the county. Dahlia felt compelled to share her equity vision and expertise with up-and-coming educational leaders. In every course she taught, she infused the theme of educational equity and challenged her students to define their future role as equity leaders. Dahlia was committed to educational justice and made sure that her students were clear about her position, encouraging them to join her in her quest on behalf of the most vulnerable students.

One particular fall semester, Dahlia had an especially outgoing group of students. The majority of the students were Latino and African American. April was one of the few White students in the class. The class was energetic, engaged, and enthusiastic about learning how to become equity leaders—all of them except April.

April was punctual to class each week, was always prepared, and submitted every assignment on time. Yet her energy was negative. She never smiled, rarely made eye contact, and did not actively participate in group discussions. Rarely was her voice heard in class discussions, except for the occasional devil's advocate commentary. Generally speaking, the class concluded that "April was a pill to have in class."

What should leaders do when confronted by negative people, particularly when trying to inspire the development of equity leaders? This is the question Dahlia began to privately ponder. As the term progressed, the rest of the class began to complain that April was becoming more and more of a wet blanket in an otherwise vibrant group of educators. Week after week, more and more students started talking about April before class, at breaks, and after class. Most of the time, they spoke within earshot of Dahlia, hoping she would hear them. She did. It seemed that the more April's behavior was noticed, the worse it got.

Some students eventually brought their concern directly to Dahlia. "How is April supposed to lead for equity with that attitude?" they asked. Dahlia advised them that she was aware of the situation and was monitoring it, and suggested that the class members should concentrate on their own development as equity leaders rather than spending time criticizing a fellow student. They shared a chuckle.

WE ARE ALL MERE MORTALS, AFTER ALL

The issue with April was weighing on Dahlia. Even though Dahlia was an experienced and successful professional, she let April get under her skin. Dahlia was perplexed. How was April going to become an equity leader if she repelled others? April was really difficult to like.

Dahlia thought that April was more focused on herself than on the needs of others, a trait incompatible with those needed to promote educational justice for others. And really, the class was right. How dare she be rude in class! It was embarrassing that Dahlia's other students noticed that April's behavior was disrespectful to Dahlia as an instructor and as a human being.

A personal fact about Dahlia was that she had grown up in a tough neighborhood and was bullied frequently for being a quiet, school-focused student. It was ironic that as a young student she kept to herself a lot to avoid trouble. Now, as an equity leader, her mission was to look for trouble! (Remember chapter 1?)

Dahlia was proud that she had prepared herself with education and experience so that she no longer had to worry about being humiliated by or feeling uncomfortable around others. And yet here she was, humiliated and uncomfortable. The more the students complained to her, the more disturbed Dahlia became. She needed to deal with the situation somehow. But what should she do?

Equity Leadership Trilogy

A common saying is that there are peacetime leaders and wartime leaders. The idea is that many leaders are effective when conditions are relatively calm, but it takes a special kind of leader to tackle difficult contexts. The implication is that turning around systemic inequities requires a tough, steadfast leader with a certain stern style that movies often depict in military generals.

We assure you with 100 percent certainty that this could not be further from the truth. In fact, equity leaders exhibit the following three key characteristics.

Leadership Maturity

In chapter 1, we discussed that equity leaders derive their strength from the moral imperative to ensure that students representing every demographic group receive the premium education that only some now experience. Students require different approaches to learning in order to succeed. Equity leaders understand that people have different levels of need and that providing that *is* equity.

Some leaders make mistakes when first exercising equity muscle. The most common reason for those missteps is a lack of grounding in leadership maturity. Leadership maturity refers to having the presence to "be the adult in the room" during difficult situations. By definition, equity issues are emotionally charged. Our best work occurs when people are passionate about fairness, justice, and opportunity for all. This leads to energy that can easily become divisive, hostile, or confrontational if not facilitated with care.

When equity leaders hone leadership maturity, they are resistant (though not immune) to getting caught up in adult drama, being swayed by persuasive pressure, or getting derailed by fast-moving human dynamics. For example, in the movie *Stand and Deliver* (Menendez, 1998), teacher Jaime Escalante

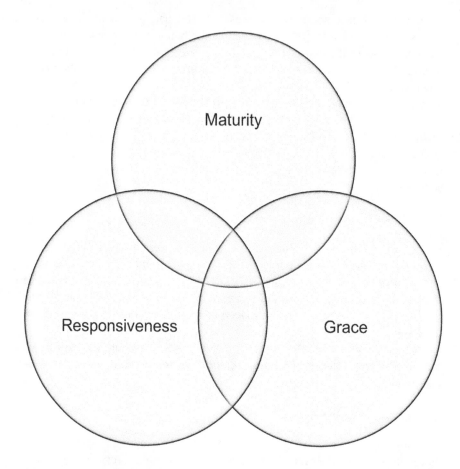

Figure 3.1.   Equity Leadership Trilogy

demonstrates high levels of leadership maturity at Garfield High School in East Los Angeles, a predominantly Latino working-class neighborhood.

The movie illustrates how a classroom teacher can be a powerful equity leader. In one memorable scene, Escalante is in a math department meeting advocating to grow the Advanced Placement calculus program at the school. In textbox 3.1 is the script for that scene. Think about what leadership maturity and immaturity look like in practice as you visualize this scene.

Escalante states his case, gives his rationale, and awaits responses. Others in the meeting are skeptical of the ability of their students to be successful in such a rigorous course. References about "these types" or "our kids can't" are invitations for equity leaders to get into the proverbial equity ring and duke it out. That did not occur in the teacher's lounge discussion at Garfield High School. It is in moments like these—"war times"—that mature equity leaders check in with their True North, take deep breaths, stay calm, and keep focused on the equity mission.

TEXTBOX 3.1. *STAND AND DELIVER* DIALOGUE

Escalante: I want to teach calculus next year.

Department Chair: Boy, that's a jump. That's ridiculous. They haven't had trigonometry or math analysis.

Escalante: They can take them this summer.

Department Chair: Our best students in summer school?

Escalante: From 7:00 to 12:00. Every day, including Saturdays. That would do it.

Department Chair: Summer classrooms are reserved for remedial courses.

Escalante: To turn this school around, you have to start from the top.

Department Chair: Mr. Escalante, don't lecture us. Our kids can't handle calculus. We don't even have the books.

Escalante: If they pass the Advanced Placement test, they get college credit.

Department Chair: There are some teachers here . . . who couldn't pass the Advanced Placement test.

Principal: You think you can make this fly?

Escalante: I teach calculus or . . . have a good day.

Department Chair: If this man can walk in here . . . and dictate his own terms, over my objections . . . I see no reason to continue as department chair.

Escalante: Don't take this personally. I'm thinking about those kids.

> Department Chair: If they try and don't succeed . . . you'll shatter what little self-confidence they have. These aren't the types that bounce back. [She walks toward the exit door.]
>
> Escalante: Have a good day.

Dahlia did not exhibit leadership maturity. Unlike Escalante, she allowed her personal experience to color her view of the situation. She also fell victim to allowing other voices to get her worked up and lose objectivity. This is leadership immaturity in practice. The problem with this is that leaders lose their ability to inspire equity action in others if they compromise their clarity of thought and measured responses in this way.

Leadership Responsiveness

The power of leadership responsiveness cannot be overstated. We know that the nature of equity work creates fertile soil for tension and conflict. This is expected because inequity discussions stomp on many long-held beliefs and values. Avoidance of conflict is a counterproductive behavior that we frequently see from leaders. The longer equity issues are avoided, the more they fester and the more difficult they are to resolve. Equity solutions take a back seat to the conflict.

The first step in leadership responsiveness is for leaders to develop an ability to read emotions, both their own and those of people they work with. This does not mean that leaders are necessarily touchy-feely. (The thought of that being a requirement would send some personality types running for the hills!) Rather, as a first step, effective leaders actively look for traces of emotion as an indication of how people are processing information or interactions. As one experienced equity mentor whispered to an aspiring equity leader who stuck to a presentation script while the audience walked out: "Don't be a rock! Read the room!" Some people are more intuitive about this than others, but the ability to interpret signs of emotion is critical and must be and can be developed.

The second step in leadership responsiveness is to modify your approach based on the emotional read. It is astounding how infrequently this occurs and how limiting this misstep is to an equity agenda. Looking to the field of medicine to objectify this concept, imagine that someone is experiencing a life-threatening condition. Imagine now that the person's entire family is in the hospital room when the doctor comes to deliver the news. For the first time, the doctor sees the person's confused five-year-old child, the terrified spouse, the anxious parents, and the stoic matriarch of the family with her own visible health issues. Then there is the patient, exhausted but hoping for good news.

How should this consult proceed? What should the doctor say and not say, show and not show, do and not do? Atul Gawande (2007), the keen observer of medical practice, reminds us that "[i]n this work against sickness, *we begin not with genetic or cellular interactions, but with human ones*" (81-82). The same is true in any field. So how should the doctor handle the consult?

Applying leadership responsiveness, the doctor spends a few minutes interacting with the family and patient, sensing their mental and emotional readiness for the news she has to share. She tailors the information appropriately, providing only general information given the wide range of family members and keenly observing their responses as she chooses her words. Then she privately consults with the patient to collaborate on how best to proceed in a way that would make the patient feel most supported. This is responsiveness in the midst of tension.

Here again, Dahlia fell short on several counts. She was very clear that the majority of the class did not like April. However, she missed three critical reads:

1. Why was the class so willing to turn on a classmate?
2. What about Dahlia made her so susceptible to the class drama?
3. Oh, and by the way—might there be an explanation for April's demeanor other than "she is a pill"?

Since Dahlia did not ask or answer these questions for herself, she landed on "April is a pill." This created a barrier for Dahlia in applying leadership responsiveness, which was a huge missed opportunity to improve the situation for everyone.

Leadership Grace

The third piece of the equity leadership trilogy is leadership grace. In this context, *grace* refers to the gift of support a leader offers someone, whether they deserve it or not, and whether others agree or not. This requires a leader to:

- value the need for work *with* others;
- prioritize the equity mission above personal comfort; and
- find strength in humility.

Textbox 3.2 lists examples of the different forms leadership grace can take.

TEXTBOX 3.2. EXAMPLES OF LEADERSHIP GRACE

- An unexpected or unwarranted favor
- Goodwill following strained interactions
- Forgiveness of a mistake
- Leniency after a misstep
- Pardon of an offense
- Empathy for poor behavior or bad decisions

The situation with April humbled Dahlia. She realized that even she, a proud equity leader, was ill equipped to handle this conflict. Early on, Dahlia considered having a private chat with April to try to counsel her, but the moment never seemed appropriate and the issue quickly escalated. Also, while Dahlia asked the class members to squash their criticism, her comments to them were light-hearted admonitions and not appeals for them to give grace to a classmate. The fleeting thought of giving April grace in any form never materialized. The tension escalated quickly through the term.

THE SHOWDOWN (OR NOT)

Finally, the last day of the course arrived. Students got ready to present equity projects they had worked on at their schools throughout the semester. The mood was so light and positive that it felt almost as if everyone skipped to class. There was great anticipation as students prepared to share their work with their colleagues, who by now had become friends.

Then April entered the room, not early but right on time. Her expression was even more blank than usual. As she took her seat, Dahlia began the class, and before anyone could complete a sentence, April spoke: "I want to present first." Dahlia could not miss the class's reaction. The other students took offense to April's seeming impertinence, though April seemed oblivious to them. Dahlia agreed to have April present first, but she was going to open class with a brief lecture. April shifted in her seat with open displeasure. The class expressed even more open contempt by rolling their eyes and sighing.

After a twenty-minute lecture summarizing highlights of the course, Dahlia gave the class a short break before the presentations. She asked everyone to leave the room. Then Dahlia walked over to April and whispered to her a request that she remain in the room for a few minutes. Dahlia told herself that this was the moment. As a teacher of educational leadership, it was her duty to confront April about her behavior.

Dahlia imagined herself asking April to reflect on how she comes across. She saw herself asking pointed questions and jogging April out of her sullen demeanor. April was either going to realize on her own that her behavior had a negative effect on people around her or Dahlia was going to tell her directly. It had been a long semester and this confrontation was a long time coming.

Leaders who commit to an equity agenda are often involved in or witness tense interactions. Even experienced equity leaders spend their careers honing their skills translating the leadership trilogy into equity action.

Find the Love

This equity action is offered without apology for its touchy-feely nature because it is so important. An absolute truism is that leaders cannot inspire people they do not connect with on a human level. Leaders cannot inspire people they do not care for, find appreciation for, or like.

We all know people who make themselves very difficult to like! But, as one leadership coach advised a district director struggling with a group of stubborn principals: "When people are most distasteful, that's when you must step up your game. Say to yourself, 'At the very least, their mother must love them! What is it about them that their momma loves? Now I must find the love!'"

Engaging in this self-talk forces a much needed smile and brings the struggle to a human level. Take a deep breath and remember this is not about you; it is about the future of our young people, especially those who are now marginalized. Equity leaders must keep their eye on the prize!

IT'S HARD TO HATE UP CLOSE

Once April and Dahlia were alone in the room, Dahlia was about to launch into her coaching session, fueled by the other students' animosity and her own personal biases. Just then, a little voice inside of Dahlia told her to hold back. Sitting across from April, Dahlia saw a vulnerability she had never noticed. It surprised Dahlia, but she felt a connection to April for the first time, if only slightly. "Are you okay?" is all Dahlia could muster.

Demonstrate Empathy

Unlike sympathy, which can be perceived as having pity for someone, *empathy* is putting yourself in someone's shoes and trying to share his or her experience. This distinction is key in an equity context, even for the ways we interact with vulnerable students. No change comes from feeling sorry for people's circumstances, and it is insulting to be on the receiving end of pity.

How did Dahlia handle her situation? When April did not readily respond to her question, Dahlia realized something was very wrong and asked, "Can I help somehow?" April's eyes welled up and she began, in a very low, monotone voice, to share a very personal story. April's twenty-one-year-old daughter had been killed by a sixteen-year-old driver in a hit-and-run exactly one year ago that day.

April had started a foundation to educate parents and teens about the dangers of allowing inexperienced teen drivers behind the wheel prematurely. She believed that it was fundamentally wrong to have the same driver training requirements for young drivers as for adults. Her foundation was trying to pass legislation that required young drivers to drive with licensed adults for at least two years before being allowed to get behind the wheel by themselves.

That evening, April was headed to the fund-raising banquet where her precious daughter was being remembered. She was to address the audience, tell her story, and ask for their support on her proposed legislation. All this was to occur after she finished with class. The room was silent, and Dahlia could not contain her tears.

April never shed a tear; her eyes were steely and fixed. Dahlia asked April, "Why are you here? Please, go to your event." April replied, "No. I have a responsibility to meet the requirements of this course. I am committed to learning everything you have to teach. Educational justice is important to me. If I can just present my final project first, I will leave after listening to as many student presentations as possible. I have to meet my obligation to you and to this class."

Situate Yourself inside the Problem

Equity leadership requires humility. However, dedication to promoting justice for vulnerable students requires leaders to ask themselves the following questions when difficulties with people arise:

- What is my part in this?
- Did I play a role in the difficulty?
- Could I have done anything differently to improve the outcome?
- Is there anything I can do now to improve the situation?
- What changes do I need to make in my behavior and practices?

A TOUGH LESSON

Just then, the class began to file in, looking at Dahlia for signs that April had finally gotten what was coming to her. In that instant, Dahlia reflected on her own leadership immaturity in how she handled this situation with the class during the semester. She was remorseful for not checking in with April earlier. She should have known something was amiss. This would have avoided lots of misperceptions and emotional distress among Dahlia and the students.

- Why did she allow the class to stir up drama about another member of the class?
- Worst of all were the questions that haunted her for years to come: What is it about *me* that did not allow April to feel comfortable enough to tell me what she was experiencing? What about *me* did not allow April to ask me for support?

When class resumed, Dahlia asked April to present her project. The class was surprised at the depth and complexity of her project, and at how her equity heart shone through her entire presentation. After she finished and the class was done asking questions, Dahlia had the class take one more brief break so that she could privately ask April to go on to her event. April reluctantly agreed. "One more thing," said Dahlia. "Would you mind if I shared your story with your classmates? I think we would all like to support your legislation." April said that would be fine, and she left.

Share Your Own Story

When the class walked back into the room and the other door was just closing behind April, they began to ask where she was going and why she was leaving early. Dahlia sat on a stool in front of the class and asked for their undivided attention. The class was riveted as Dahlia told April's story.

"April agreed to let me share her story with you in the event that you'd like to support her proposed legislation," she said. The class was too choked up to speak. Dahlia continued, "but I wanted to tell you because I am ashamed. I am ashamed of my thoughts and behavior and that I allowed you all to respond in kind. The lesson here is that everyone has a story."

Dahlia went on to explain that equity leadership is a difficult pursuit. We need to work through and with others to make change happen. We are all different, and it is impossible to know what life experiences people have had that color their perspectives. She explained that her personal experiences in school clouded her ability to be effective with April. Students joined in the conversation and were ashamed to share that they attributed April's strange behaviors to the fact that she was the only nonminority student in the class. They thought she might not be ready or that she was uncomfortable to do what was necessary to lead an equity agenda for Latino and African American students. Their rush to judgment was wrong.

Research in cognitive psychology teaches us that in the absence of understanding, the human brain makes meaning. This is an ever-present danger when interacting with people on sensitive issues. When people behave in ways we do not understand, it is natural to leap to making interpretations of those behaviors through our own prism. But that is highly subject to unconscious bias. In other words, we make up stories to explain people we do not understand, but in doing so, we make judgments that are often not based in fact (Fiarman, 2016). Stereotyping and imposing personal biases are a real likelihood.

- What was it about Dahlia's students that led to the conflict with April?
- Would their response to April have been different if they had accurate information?
- What if April were not the sole White student? Would things have been different?
- Was there an underlying belief that only minorities can be authentic equity leaders?
- What if they showed some of the characteristics of the leadership trilogy?

The best leaders allow for people to be people without adding additional meaning to that. We all have stories; we all have good days and bad days. We hope that our leaders appreciate that and allow us to get ourselves back on track in our own way. Let us all strive to become leaders who remember that *everyone* has a story.

Dahlia went home that evening so thankful that she listened to her inner voice and did not confront April, as she had planned. Instead, that evening became a powerful leadership lesson for the class, and one of the most profound learning experiences for Dahlia as she herself grew as an equity leader.

EQUITY HOOK: EVERYONE'S GOT A STORY

SUMMARY

This chapter focuses on key characteristics equity leaders must have to effectively navigate difficult adult interactions that inevitably arise in equity work. The equity leader in this case, Dahlia, was tested by a member of her class with a difficult personality. What Dahlia thought would be a teachable moment for others became a personal lesson for herself. April, the difficult personality, had a story.

When faced with these challenging situations, we recommend that equity leaders become "the adult in the room" and embrace an equity leadership trilogy:

- Leadership maturity
- Leadership responsiveness
- Leadership grace

Equity leaders must inspire, find empathy, and exhibit humility. Dahlia's leadership lesson evolved from her willingness to reflect and open her mind and heart to hear the story of another. This case also highlights how we all have conscious and unconscious biases about people that are often based on their demographic characteristics. Those biases may—and often do—lead to misguided judgments about a person's behavior, motivation, and beliefs. They can also lead to hurtful judgments about entire groups of people.

This chapter ends with the argument that equity leaders need to appreciate that everyone has a story, and that investing in knowing one another is critical to leading equity work. Taking time to know one another is critical, especially during conflict, because it is hard to hate up close.

EQUITY CONCEPTS

- *Equity Leadership Trilogy:* These are three of the most critical traits that impactful equity leaders exhibit.

  - *Leadership maturity:* This level of leadership development makes it clear that the leader is always "the level-headed adult in the room."
  - *Leadership responsiveness:* Leaders who master this capacity are able to:

    - read subtle signs of human emotion, and
    - turn that reading into data to inform modified leadership action.

  - *Leadership grace:* The most effective equity leaders have the humility to grant people a pass or goodwill even when they "don't deserve it."

EQUITY ACTIONS

- Find the love. Commit to identifying a redeeming quality in every person with whom you interact, no matter how difficult an individual may be. Be open to establishing authentic relationships with those you hope to lead and inspire.

- Demonstrate empathy. Put yourself in the emotional shoes of people you are leading to better appreciate their perspectives. Empathize, but do not sympathize, which can be perceived as pity and can be insulting.
- Situate yourself inside the problem. Reflect on challenging interactions with people and ask yourself what role *you* played in the tension, what *you* could have done differently to effect a better outcome, and what *you* can do now to improve the situation.
- Share your own story. Equity leadership puts educators at constant risk of being challenged or even disliked. Be vulnerable with people by sharing aspects of your life experience that color your perspective, because the idea that it is hard to hate up close works both ways.

Chapter Four

Inspiring Equity Action

Equity Hook: Lead with a Flashlight, Not a Club

Have you ever wondered . . .

- What is the *most* effective way for leaders to inspire people to embrace equity proposals?
- What is the *least* effective way to lead equity work?
- Why people do not agree on what is true, even in the face of data and facts?
- How to navigate sticky situations when people resist equity-promoting changes?

Very few leaders *intentionally* try to beat people into submission mentally and emotionally. Really! Yet they—we—may do just that without realizing it. The not-so-obvious meaning of this Equity Hook, "lead with a flashlight, not a club," was experienced firsthand by Rita, the head counselor at Bright High School (BHS).

A kind person by nature, Rita took her responsibilities as leader of the guidance department very seriously. She fully appreciated the life-changing role that high school counselors play in the lives of young people and welcomed the opportunity to inspire the counseling team to go the extra mile for students.

BHS is a large urban high school in a high-poverty area. The school worked hard for years to improve its graduation rate and was proud to boast that 80 percent of its freshmen graduated four years later. This was a huge improvement over the previous 50 percent graduation rate.

Chapter 4

CLOSE, BUT NO PRIZE

Rita was pleased at this improvement, but was troubled that even though they graduated, most students did not include higher education in their plans for their lives after graduation. It hurt her heart to know that only 18 percent of seniors graduated eligible to apply to a four-year university. The school had worked hard on graduation rates, but put very little effort into preparing students for college.

Rita knew the power of education to transform lives because she was a first-generation college student herself. She was the first in her family to earn a bachelor's degree, but not the last. In fact, after she went to college, her siblings, cousins, and nieces and nephews did the same, and their entire family was in a much better place—economically, socially, and even physically—as a result.

Rita spoke to her principal about her concerns and received full support to lead the counseling team on an initiative to improve the four-year college eligibility rate for graduates of BHS. The principal thought Rita would be the perfect person to lead the effort because the strength of her conviction was perfectly balanced by her warm personality.

This seemed like an ideal combination for collaborating with counselors to better align their practices to the college eligibility goal. Rita went back to the counseling office and called a meeting of her colleagues. They always responded to her requests because she spoke to them with respect and treated them as professionals.

ALL PEOPLE DON'T THINK LIKE ME?

Rita shared her personal story about college and the transformative effect her education had on her and her entire family. Then she proposed that the counseling team take up a new charge to ensure that upon graduation from BHS, all students have as many options as possible, including attendance at a university.

Rita was surprised to receive mixed reactions. She believed that the counselors were all good people, but some just did not support the goal to graduate all students four-year university eligible. They became upset and repeated the statistic in their accreditation plan that 85 percent of their students go on to college. Rita corrected them, sharing that only 18 percent graduated eligible for four-year institutions, and only half of those actually enrolled as freshmen the next year. The rest of the students enrolled in local community colleges.

The louder voices on the team argued the merits of the community college for their students. It gave students time to grow academically and socially before they transferred to a four-year university. The campuses were close to home and affordable. Rita offered up for discussion the poor transfer rates from their local community colleges.

OH SAY, CAN YOU SEE NOW?

Rita knew from a National Student Clearinghouse report (2016) that only 6 percent of BHS graduates who started at the community college graduated with a bachelor's degree within six years. Only 6 percent! The six-year bachelor's degree rate for BHS students starting at four-year institutions was much better, though it was still only 45 percent.

Rita also shared—from national statistics and from her own personal experience—the significant differences in average lifestyle of a person with a bachelor's degree versus one without a degree. First, there is about a $24,000 difference in annual median salary between high school graduates and their peers with bachelor's degrees, a salary difference between about $3,000 a month and $5,000 a month. *That* is a lifestyle difference!

Rita, who had personally experienced the standard of living advantages of having a degree, had prepared notes on the related lifestyle benefits of a four-year degree taken from a College Board report (Ma, Pender, & Welsh, 2016), including:

- Sixty-nine percent of college graduates, as opposed to 45 percent of high school graduates, reported exercising each week vigorously.
- Thirty-nine percent of those with a bachelor's degree performed some type of volunteer service to help the community in 2015, as opposed to 16 percent of those with a high school diploma.
- Forty-five percent of college graduates voted in the 2014 midterm election, compared with 20 percent of high school graduates in the same age group.
- The children of college graduates were more likely to be involved in a variety of educational activities with their families.

There! They *had* to see now. But this was not the case. Rita tried her best to nonjudgmentally listen to all the reasons why BHS students need not be held to the higher academic standard expected of more privileged students. The counselors completely ignored the data Rita presented. She was saddened and disappointed that two counselors who she knew agreed with her sat quietly through the meeting. She was alone.

WHO ARE THEY TALKING ABOUT?

As the discussion continued, some counselors stated that not many BHS students were "college material." They argued that many of "these types of students" lacked the work ethic, academic ability, parental support, or interest in higher education. They said that the students' culture did not value education. Rita asked the counselor team if they *all* felt that way. Two counselors out of the seven said they did not agree; however, they made it a point to emphasize that they fully respected their colleagues' right to their opinion.

Rita had the notion that these counselors might be experiencing some peer pressure. They had to work with these colleagues every day! Other counselors quickly listed students by name who were examples of those who were appropriately programmed into graduation-only courses.

At this point, Rita realized that this would be only the first of many badly needed conversations about expectations and outcomes, but she wisely ended this first meeting early. She thanked the team for so openly expressing their thoughts and encouraged them to continue thinking about the proposed change. She gave them each a warm smile as they left the meeting room.

When Rita got back to her office, she began to feel strained and almost teary as the words of some of the counselors grated on her conscience. What did they mean all students aren't "college material"? What if some counselor had said that about her when she was a student? *Had* they? What culture does not value education? Her concern turned to frustration and then to anger.

She decided she needed data, and she began to pull up the transcripts of a random group of seniors. Rita needed to find out if the data could help her to better understand why so few students were graduating college ready. She believed that all BHS students deserved to graduate college ready and were capable of participating in the more rigorous academic programs. Her hunch was that there was some systemic reason to explain the results. What she found from the transcripts was maddening.

EDUCATING RITA

In her review of the transcripts, Rita discovered two clear patterns:

1. Some students were struggling in every subject, with low grades peppered throughout their entire career at BHS. The appropriate plan for these students was to help them graduate from high school.
2. But more often than not, students who were well on their way to completing the college-prep sequence stopped at some point—mostly in their junior or senior year. In fact, most students missed completing

the sequence by only one or two classes! These students were so close! Rita thought these data certainly dispelled the myth that these students were not academically capable!

Rita could not wait to share what she learned with the counselors because she just knew their thinking would be transformed. So she held an impromptu counseling meeting the following day. She shared the transcripts and her analysis and then opened the meeting for discussion. Interestingly, those two counselors who were quietly supportive of the vision before became a bit more openly excited. But those counselors who were resistant became more vocal in their opposition to expecting all students to graduate college ready. What could possibly explain these extreme reactions?

Confirmation Bias

How can it be that faced with irrefutable facts, people still do not agree on a position? A counterintuitive psychological phenomenon is that opinions people hold are almost impervious to change. Even in the face of facts, data, or examples, people's opinions are virtually unalterable. In fact, the more facts, data, or examples presented, the more stubborn some people become in holding their opinions. How is this possible? Bias—but not the way people often think of bias.

Confirmation bias is a predisposition that humans have for seeking data to support their particular point of view. This is a subconscious cognitive process, not a strategy of devious people looking to defend a position. One of the best examples of confirmation bias is a study published in *Pediatrics Journal* (Nyhab, Reifler, Richey, & Freed, 2014; also cited in Avelar La Salle, Johnson, & Maldonado French, 2014).

The study explored parents' concerns about immunizing newborns and the effectiveness of provaccination campaigns. Parents were given either data, compliance information, or emotional appeals to persuade them of the importance of vaccinations. But here's the shocker. Regardless of the messaging, vaccine-averse parents not only did not change their minds, they became even more determined not to vaccinate their children. These campaigns had no effect on public opinion. *None.*

How could that be? After all, what reasonable person would not find data, regulations, or emotional pleas persuasive? The findings of this study have a message for equity leaders whose job it is to inspire people to think differently in order to transform schools and districts to better serve all students. The study is actually a fundamental critique of how all of us operate at every level in education. Take a moment to process that.

How often do we find ourselves trying to sway public opinion or, conversely, being the target of a campaign to influence our thinking? No matter what our job as educators is, we strive to improve conditions for students. This requires us to update and change our practices constantly. We must be flexible in our thinking. Each time we engage someone, we are sharing our ideas, beliefs, and opinions. Whether we are conscious of it or not, we are trying to influence that person's way of thinking, quite often trying to sway them to our way of thinking.

This has called into question a few tried-and-true strategies that we believe are now worth sharing as cautionary tales. As educators, usually our first go-to is the scientific approach.

People with bachelor's degrees earn over $24,000 more than those without degrees.

This kind of evidence-based information should work! It is researched and supported by data. And yet, despite such compelling evidence, reasonable people often don't always see eye to eye, as in Rita's case.

If this approach is not successful, we might move to the "because I said so" default: *Federal guidelines require . . .* or *the Accreditation Team recommendation necessitates that we make university eligibility a school goal.* Who wouldn't want to follow regulations? Surely, we believe that they're in the best interest of students, right? Well, it turns out that not everyone trusts the rules, and some of us even resent them.

Next, we might try appealing to emotion. The story of Kyle, described in the preface of this book, is a true story about a boy who began kindergarten like most other students, but systemic educational decisions that were meant to help him wound up trapping him in a low-performing track year after year. The result was tragic.

Kyle came to realize that his high expectations for himself clashed with the limited opportunities afforded him by his schooling, so he eventually dropped out. His experience should cause us *all* to think about the schooling decisions—small and large—that we make for students throughout their educational careers. While it should persuade every one of us, beyond a shadow of a doubt, that tracking is simply wrong, not everyone arrives at the same conclusion—which brings us back to the vaccination study.

- Why had none of the communication approaches worked?
- And why do our best presentations—riddled with data, research, stories, and pictures—not bring us all into agreement about how to move ahead?
- If the primary ways we know to communicate have no effect, then how do those of us who are entrusted with the education of the nation's children move our institutions forward?
- How can we evolve, grow, and improve if our minds are stuck?

The reason the parents rejected the information about vaccinations was confirmation bias. People behave in accordance with their belief systems: *We are our beliefs.* Our beliefs form our identity. Changing parents' opinions on the benefits of vaccinations would require an admission that they were harming their newborns, implying that they were bad parents. That was too painful a notion, and so they found reasons to reject the information, whether by challenging its veracity, related political agenda, or credibility of the messengers, or by finding isolated examples to support their position. Sound familiar?

To Rita's counselors, who were accustomed to a certain guidance process, a statement such as, "This other approach is better" could be interpreted as, "I have not been a good counselor; I've been harming my students." Since this is too painful to accept, they applied confirmation bias and found a host of tangential points to support their current practice.

BACK TO THE DRAWING BOARD

Back at her desk, Rita thought about dropping the entire issue. But as a true equity leader, her True North gave her the strength and conviction to persist. When equity leaders get knocked down, they get up, dust themselves off, and continue to focus on their Equity True North. They are committed to achieving equity for their students and continue to search out ways and people to make that happen.

So Rita continued to ponder her situation. A question ran through her mind. She wondered if there existed any relationship between the beliefs expressed by the counselors and the course-placement decisions they made for students. Rita pulled random student transcripts from each counselor's caseload and repeated her analysis. Her worst fears were confirmed when she saw that individual counselors were imposing their own internal rules in programming students, and that those rules aligned well with their stated beliefs about students and their college potential.

Two counselors had college expectations for their students and clearly pushed them as far as they could. When students received a D in math during the regular school year, these counselors enrolled them in summer school so that they could take and be better prepared for the more advanced math course the following year. The same counselors repeated these kinds of personal decisions over and over for most of their students. These decisions were not random; they followed an internal rule system that said, "What can I do to encourage students to hit that university eligible bar?"

In contrast, other counselors followed different internal rule systems that appeared to say, "What can I do to make sure students graduate?" Transcript after transcript indicated that their students could have continued on the college-prep path, but at some point stopped. Many transcripts showed that students who earned a C in biology, for instance, ended their science course sequence at that point, having taken enough science credits for graduation. Such students would have graduated four-year college eligible with just one or two more science classes. Transcripts from these counselors' caseloads indicated one missed opportunity after another.

MORE AND BETTER DATA SHOULD HELP

Rita decided to create a table of her findings for her team. She was attempting to shed more light on the issues by unpacking more data. Surely, she thought, this would create food for deep discussion. Across the top were the college eligibility requirements, and along the vertical axis was listed each counselor's name with the percentage of his or her senior caseload that had graduated university eligible for the past three years. The table clearly demonstrated that some counselors made decisions that propelled students toward college eligibility, while others did not.

She decided to hold another counseling meeting the next day to share the data. At the meeting, she handed out a sheet to each counselor with the table that showed all the student placement patterns for all counselors' caseloads. Before they digested the information, she began to interpret the data for them, asking thought-provoking questions as she went along.

The mood quickly became defensive, and some counselors walked out of the meeting upset. Even the two counselors who agreed with Rita walked out in support of their friends. Everyone felt uncomfortable. The counselors were demonstrating their informal power to resist the changes that Rita was pushing. Even though there was evidence that some were more equity minded and aligned with an equity agenda, peer pressure functioned as an informal power structure within the department. What was our equity leader's next move?

Confused by the counselors' reaction and still persistent, Rita sought out her principal for advice. After listening to her story, he said, "You are a natural leader and have always enjoyed the high regard of people you work with."

Very upset, Rita said, "Yes, but this time they reacted like I hit them over the head or something! All of them acted that way. But they know me!"

"It is true, Rita. You do not club when you lead . . . normally. But this time, you did." *What?* He explained that leaders often make this error. Clubs are in the eye of the beholder—that is, whether people are threatened is measured by their feelings, not our intentions. (This is akin to the idea that whether teaching is effective depends on how well students learn, not how well the teacher executed a lesson plan.)

Even though Rita's personality was collaborative and respectful, she whacked the group hard with the data she offered, so hard that they could not receive the message about equity that she wanted to share. The principal noted that although she did not mean it, Rita had misread the situation by failing to consider natural human reactions prior to engaging them.

Change Aversion

It is way too easy to be suspect of people's motives when they block what we believe is an important equity plan. Equity leaders may imagine that those who do not instantly join up do not care enough about their students to make necessary changes. In truth, a second psychological phenomenon applies here. *Change aversion* is a safety mechanism of the human brain. Humans are constantly on watch for potential threats, and the brain will often register proposed changes to routines as possible threats.

Rita's principal shared that a wise director he worked with years before had given him the best advice: As difficult as it may be, before you ask people to change anything, put yourself in their shoes and imagine yourself on your worst day.

- What previous experiences might this trigger for you?
- How might it make you feel?
- What might pass through your mind?

Equity leaders are constantly in a position of "looking for trouble" (see chapter 1) to disrupt inequitable systems and improve outcomes for students. By definition, then, equity leaders are at the center of change. When leading equity initiatives, remember that many people will naturally react with fear about how the change could affect them personally.

We wish everyone could be such a committed advocate of educational justice that no one would prioritize their personal comfort over equity initiatives. However, this is simply not natural. Some people do behave that way, but they are truly exceptional.

Table 4.1 represents some of the threats that people could perceive in the midst of considering a change to comfortable routines.

Here is a key point: Human biases are the result of biological, psychological, and socialization processes and are not necessarily a character flaw. Are there people whose biases are deliberate manifestations of racist, antisocial, or otherwise hurtful ideologies? Of course. But equity leaders trying to disrupt legacy systems are much better served presuming positive intent and viewing bias as a human trait that all people have in some form or another (Fiarman, 2016). This stance allows leaders to demonstrate empathy and interact with people on sticky topics without the weight of judgment and criticism as a barrier.

Should the fact that humans tend to be change averse stop equity leaders from working to create equitable systems to help students? Heck no! What

Table 4.1.   Change Aversion Examples

Threat	Self-Talk *"If I accept this change . . ."*
Fear of Failure	I may expose what I don't know about the topic. People will think less of me.
Obsolescence	People may notice that I am not up-to-date on tools, practices, or current thinking in my field. I may be perceived as a dinosaur and become less valued.
Loss of Autonomy	I may be in the position where others will be more involved in my work. They might think that my work should be better, which would be embarrassing and would lead to closer scrutiny of my work.
Diminished Livelihood	I may not be up to the challenge and be identified as a deficient employee, which could affect my employment and financial security.
Challenged Belief Systems	I may have to become involved in discussions about sensitive topics that make me feel nervous because I don't agree with others and I may be labeled in some negative way.

this understanding does is help leaders better understand and prepare for the human reaction to change initiatives. It also relieves the burden of thinking ill of people who are not immediately excited about change proposals. Thoughts like that are draining, unproductive, and often not accurate once we understand a bit about the human brain.

Rita consulted once again with her principal on the status of the equity plan. Could Rita find a way to continue her equity quest after she had pounded the counseling team? After some contemplation, she moved ahead with the following action steps.

Demonstrate Humility

Relationships are the real bricks and mortar in any institution. Rita needed to repair her relationship with the counseling team. She decided to visit the counselors individually in their offices. She acknowledged her clumsy attempt to bring forward an equity issue, then apologized for making them feel uncomfortable. She said that she knew that each counselor was operating in the way he or she sincerely thought was best for their students. Each counselor thanked her and seemed to feel much better after her visit.

Build on Past Successes

Lead equity initiatives by fully acknowledging and describing current conditions that are aligned with the new direction, rather than the gaps. In other words, start by celebrating what is good at the moment. This may take some digging, but there is always something to acknowledge, no matter how small.

Rita accomplished this by reconvening the counseling team to reset. She asked the team to enumerate all the changes they had participated in during their time at BHS that were benefiting their students. The major source of pride was the amazing increase in graduation rate. Rita asked the team to recall their thoughts about the 100 percent graduation initiative when it was initially proposed.

- What previous experiences did it trigger for you?
- How did it make you feel?
- What thoughts passed through your mind?

The positive tone was palpable as the counselors recalled their before-and-after experiences with the graduation initiative. They had come so far! The team was able to articulate thoughts that were examples of both confirmation bias and threat aversion, as demonstrated in table 4.2.

Rita asked the team to draw a line graph illustrating the graduation rate each year for the past five years. The drawing demonstrated dramatic gains, from 50 percent to 80 percent. The following discussion sounded like this:

Table 4.2. Language Samples of Cognitive Bias

Prompt: How did you feel when the goal for 100 percent graduation at BHS was introduced?

Confirmation Bias	*Threat Aversion*
At first I was worried because I knew lots of students over the years who could not meet the graduation requirements. Remember James, Heather, Letty, . . . ?	I was worried that my evaluation would be tied to the graduation rate of my students.
We had tried to improve the grad rate before but the students were not on board, so we moved away from that as a priority. The second time it came up, I thought it would be the same thing.	I couldn't imagine how I was supposed to keep such close tabs on all my students with such a large caseload. It was scary.
I worked so hard with one student but she ended up dropping out anyway, so when the 100 percent grad goal was brought up, I was really not on board at first.	I just knew that administration was going to hang around our guidance office to see if we were doing things the way they wanted. I had my own system of working with students that was working for me.

Do you remember Jennifer? I thought she'd never make it! I almost cried at her graduation.

Yes, she was in your office almost every day, it seemed. What did you do for her?

Really, she just needed help staying focused. I did grade checks with her and helped her stay organized.

Yes, my challenges were the Barton twins. Remember them?

Of course. Those boys were a ball of energy!

Well, not all staff members appreciated that energy! I spent a lot of time just visiting their teachers or running interference for them with other staff members. They just needed a little help from someone in their corner.

Reframe the Challenge as an Opportunity

Rita asked the team to share updates on what former students were doing now, after graduation. Every counselor had maintained communication with several graduates who had lifestyle advantages because of their high school graduation.

On the heels of the pride over their success in improving graduation rates, Rita posed food for thought. In a rather regal tone, she said, "Esteemed counseling team, let us open up our imaginations once again. Let us think of Jennifer, the Barton twins, and your other graduates.

- What *could* their lives be like if they had bachelor's degrees?
- What could their lives be like five, ten, and fifteen years from now *with* a degree compared to without?"

By reframing the potentially threatening challenge as an opportunity, Rita watched the team move away from their personal concerns and toward equity-centered possibility thinking. As she observed the team, she could actually visualize the energy move away from the threat site of their brain (the small amygdala near the temporal lobe) to imagination and dream sprinkles all over the brain! (Rita has a vivid imagination.)

This equity action is particularly effective in groups where different voices and insights can ping off one another.

Shine a Light on Relatable Models

A picture is worth a thousand words. This equity action is a takeoff on that notion. We know that people fear the unknown. Helping people learn about, visit, watch in action, or talk to others who have experienced the change being proposed can have profound effects on helping people gain comfort with a new idea.

Here is one important caveat: Examples and models must be relatable. People must be able to see themselves in the examples: similar students, staff, conditions, and so on. Otherwise, models will be dismissed as out of hand. *This* is the point when data should be introduced. Couple exposure to models with outcome data and results only after the foundation is laid by discussing the previous action steps.

Rita shared examples of similar schools' efforts to increase college eligibility rates and focused on celebrating the success of the models. She invited the team to visit those schools, call their counselors, and read about schools making growth in college eligibility rates. Then she gently revisited the gap between the outcomes at BHS and the models. She left data on individual counselor placement patterns for private conversations at this stage. Not every counselor accepted her invitation to learn from these models, but some did.

Grow Methodically

At a subsequent meeting, Rita again shared her pride in the fact that the counseling department had led the graduation campaign that improved rates from 50 to 80 percent in the previous five years. Thousands of student lives were forever improved because of the efforts of the counselors.

Next Rita revisited her goal to work with the team on something significant to improve the lives of their students and community even more. She shared her family history and the transformative power of her education to her life, as well as that of her immediate and extended family. Others chimed in as well. Rita said, "Let's work together to give all of our students the opportunity that we got to become college eligible. Then students can choose what they want to do after graduation from every available option, up to and including university attendance, just like students in higher-income areas."

Rita suggested that they spend the rest of the school year piloting new processes with the senior class, perfect their system, and then go schoolwide the following year. Ultimately, four counselors agreed to try the pilot. When she spoke to the resistant counselors, she said, "I see that we disagree that all students should have the opportunity to graduate college ready. For now, we will have to respectfully agree to disagree. But we will move forward, and as we do, I promise to be sensitive to the fact that you will be implementing something you are not totally comfortable with, and I will appreciate your sincere attempts to try."

This transition was not always smooth, but over five years the college-going rate increased remarkably, from 18 to 48 percent. It is important to note that not all counselors who began the initiative were still there five years later. Some made the personal decision to transfer or retire. One was encouraged to leave the profession by the administration, for a variety of reasons. But with those who remained and the addition of some new hires, the culture of the counseling department was forever changed, and BHS systematized course-placement practices aligned with the goal of four-year-college eligibility.

Very few leaders intentionally lead in a harsh, hurtful manner, but the net effect can still be a club over the head, as demonstrated by Rita's example. Impactful equity leaders realize that changing inequitable systems requires working with people and that there is great power in leading with a flashlight and not a club—focusing on providing people with exposure to thoughts, information, examples, data, in a manner that promotes self-reflection and possibility thinking, with equity as the True North.

EQUITY HOOK: LEAD WITH A FLASHLIGHT, NOT A CLUB

SUMMARY

Chapter 4 highlights equity leadership behaviors that must be developed to transform policies and practices in settings that are resistant to change. This example demonstrates how even relational leaders can inadvertently come across in ways that feel harsh to others. This blocks the equity message and generates resistance to change.

We have discussed the need to understand what is generating the resistance and explained how the brain perceives change as a threat. We have shared some concrete strategies that are necessary to address these perceived threats *before* initiating changes. If cognitive biases are ignored, they will block any movement toward equity action.

This chapter outlines a set of action steps to move a resistant team forward with an equity vision by appreciating how the human brain processes change and working with that process rather than ignoring it.

EQUITY CONCEPTS

- *Cognitive Bias:* This is the tendency of the human brain to process experiences in predictable ways.

- *Confirmation bias:* The human tendency to seek out, remember, and focus on information that supports one's point of view.
- *Threat aversion:* The human tendency to respond to potential changes to habits and established routines as a threat.
- *Opportunity reframing:* Proposing an alternative way to view a situation from the current reality to a vision of change that is posed as an opportunity.

EQUITY ACTIONS

- Demonstrate humility. Lead authentically, without pretense, making human connections a priority.
- Build on prior successes. Thoroughly extract the lessons from and celebrate past equity successes, no matter how small, as a foundation for introducing a change initiative.
- Shine a light on relatable models. Demystify change proposals by inviting people to learn from models or examples of the change you seek through readings, personal contacts with model implementers, or visits to exemplar sites.
- Grow methodically. Avoid system-wide implementation of equity initiatives until they have been tested and systematized on a small scale first, to increase the likelihood of success.

Chapter Five

Growing an Equity Culture

Equity Hook: I Want You to Want To

Have you ever wondered . . .

• How to inspire people whose fundamental view of equity does not match yours?
• What to do when you identify inequitable practices that people are completely committed to?
• How to respond when people say outrageous things about vulnerable students in your presence?
• What is the best way to unravel inequitable practices even when you are about the only one who is concerned?

One of the most difficult challenges for equity leaders is working with people who do not share our fundamental worldview about equity. A principal discovered this when his neighborhood experienced a dramatic shift in student demographics. In the midst of equity conflict, this Equity Hook, "I want you to want to," became the tipping point that helped him navigate resistance to a change proposal. It also built the collective ownership and buy-in essential to long-term sustainability of equity initiatives.

Dr. Durán was the young principal of a successful K–6 school with a history of no major concerns—until something happened. It was his second year on the job. The district had a sudden 25 percent influx of students moving in from another neighborhood. The new student demographics were unlike those of the current student population.

A large urban area surrounding Dr. Durán's school rapidly gentrified and pushed out families who could not afford the increased rents. As the closest neighboring district with affordable housing, Dr. Durán's school became the recipient of many students whose families were forced to move from their neighborhoods. Most students were Latino and African American, and many came from low-income circumstances.

The school was welcoming of the new students. When the changes began, Dr. Durán got ahead of any possible hiccups by reminding everybody that any student who attended their school was a part of their family. A natural nurturer, Dr. Durán modeled respectful interactions with new students and families. He abided by the historical norms of the school by empowering the staff to craft a school plan to support the new students. Trust in the staff had always been a school strength.

It appeared that the staff worked hard to embrace everyone, and the established community was careful to be sensitive to the new families. Schools encouraged new families to attend school functions and made sure to include them in all their activities.

Fairly quickly, however, it became apparent that the new students and their families were different in more ways than just their demographics. They did not have the academic background that students in the district had acquired over time. Their use of language in school and academic settings was informal. Their reading and math skills were not at grade level, and their writing was weak as well.

Beyond ensuring that new families felt welcome, Dr. Durán's school did not have a strategy to address this growing academic need. The central office was largely oblivious, leaving the school to address these new conditions on its own. Therefore, the school did as schools do when they are in a jam—the educators came up with what they thought was the best approach to address the need.

WHAT'S THE PLAN, DR. DURÁN?

The principal and staff felt compelled to meet students where they were, and teachers struggled to imagine how to do this in their existing classes. So the staff opted to form new classes for students who had transferred in from other neighborhoods. Their intent was to have multi-grade classes designed to help students acclimate to the school culture and academic expectations, modeled after newcomer programs for foreign students.

Some students were assigned to these classes for part of the day; others, for the full day. Dr. Durán was not fully involved in the planning, but he believed in empowering the staff to do what was best for their students. About a month after the school year started, Dr. Durán went to visit the new classes to demonstrate administrative support and see how he might assist the teachers.

On the first class visit, in the K–1 room, he was pleased to see the teacher teaching, students learning, and staff feeling positive. He asked the teacher about the new students and discovered that she had formed intervention groups that were working very well.

On the second classroom visit, the second- and third-grade teacher shared some class highlights, which also pleased Dr. Durán. However, when the bell rang for the first break, he walked across campus and noticed that the new students playing on the yard seemed to be grouped by race and ethnicity. He did a double-take to confirm that his observation was correct and verified that students were in fact segregated on the yard. Just as he was leaving the yard, he asked the playground supervisor how he was responding to the influx of new students. "We've begun a special play program designed especially for them," he said. Dr. Durán left feeling uneasy.

Walking to the third classroom, he began to have a sinking feeling in the pit of his stomach. Not sure exactly what was distressing him, and not wanting to jump to conclusions, he pensively arrived at the next class. This time, on arrival he specifically asked the teacher how he was meeting the needs of the new students. The teacher described the reassignment of some intervention aides to support those students. Dr. Durán did what he later regretted not doing at the first two classes: He asked to sit in on the classes to actually observe the new students learning for an extended period of time. Dr. Durán held his breath as he sat down to observe the class in action, hoping to disprove his emerging equity concern.

WHAT DID DR. DURÁN SEE?

Equity leaders experience many challenges. Disrupting inequitable school systems is no joke! Frankly, even equity-oriented educators do not necessarily have sufficient background and training to effectively address challenges when they find themselves immersed in troublesome situations. Like Dr. Durán, many educators have a natural inclination toward equity, but do not have the technical clarity to describe their hunches with precision.

Dr. Durán, an equity leader in progress, had the passion and the equity heart to be concerned but needed to refine his thinking to decide what equity actions to take. His observations yielded the following insights:

- New-student classes were physically isolated far across the yard from the main campus in portable classrooms formerly used for storage.
- Some teachers who volunteered to form these classes had sincere caregiver personalities but were not necessarily models of powerful teaching and learning.
- Class schedules revealed that as much as half of the school day was devoted to developing soft skills, such as school rules, pillars of good

character, and other school culture markers mostly related to student conduct.

- Because classes were multi-grade, instruction was individualized, mostly using computer programs that students tested into by level. Therefore, grade-level instruction in core subjects was very limited.
- Following students to the yard, Dr. Durán noticed that new classes were assigned their own separate play areas.

Though it was not instant, Dr. Durán came to the realization that his school's plan for supporting new students was actually bad. In his quest to empower his staff, in keeping with the school practice, he had unwittingly abdicated his role as equity leader and now had a messy situation to deal with that was harmful to children.

Ask yourself:

- What would you do if decisions others made did not match your conception of educational equity?
- How would you respond if your goal were to protect the all-important and complex adult relationships?
- How do the most impactful educators develop into equity leaders?

Dr. Durán is an actual equity-leaning leader who faced this exact dilemma. If handled poorly, a misalignment of this sort could spin out of control and create divisiveness and infighting, the ramifications of which could last for years. If handled effectively, however, this type of quandary could become a learning experience for an entire school community, bringing all parties even closer together to focus on their True North.

The example of Dr. Durán describes a highly effective strategy for handling situations like this when you want people to want to see things through an equity lens while honoring the importance of relationships. In other words, what do you do when caught between an equity rock and an inequitable hard place?

Equity Vision

Educational leaders with equity vision must develop an equity eye. *Equity vision* is the state of being able to study a situation and discern whether and how it promotes or suppresses equitable outcomes for students.

- How do leaders develop the ability to identify equitable and inequitable practices?
- How do we learn how to respond in the interest of educational justice for all?

Equity vision requires the development of a substantive knowledge base in institutional racism and school practices that result in inequitable outcomes for students. For instance, appropriately addressing Dr. Durán's dilemma requires a historical perspective of equity concepts such as segregation in education.

A key historical theme in the history of American schooling is racial and ethnic segregation of students. A basic question is, what is the best way to educate students from different backgrounds? A deeper discussion of this topic is beyond the scope of this book. However, there are two key court decisions that all equity leaders must integrate into their historical knowledge base.

- *Brown v. Board of Education of Topeka* (1954)—Separate Is Unequal

  After a legacy of forcing African American students to attend separate schools from their White peers, this Supreme Court case outlawed the practice by overturning the 1896 *Plessy v. Ferguson* case, which had decided that "separate but equal" public facilities—including schools— were legal.

  The human story behind the case was that a father, Oliver L. Brown, was upset that his third-grade daughter, Linda, was required to walk six blocks to the bus stop to ride to her segregated Black school located a mile away from the stop. Meanwhile, a White-only school was just a few blocks from their home. What parent could not relate to Mr. Brown? Chief Justice Earl Warren wrote the opinion for the court that said in part:

  > We conclude that, in the field of public education, the doctrine of "separate but equal" has no place. Separate educational facilities are inherently unequal. Therefore, we hold that the plaintiffs and others similarly situated for whom the actions have been brought are, by reason of the segregation complained of, deprived of the equal protection of the laws guaranteed by the Fourteenth Amendment.

- *Mendez v. Westminster School District of Orange County* (1946)—Separate Is Not Equal in California

  This federal court case is not as well known as *Brown v. Board of Education* but is profoundly significant in the history of American schooling. Predating the *Brown* decision, the case took up the constitutionality of assigning students of Mexican descent to schools deemed "Mexican Schools," denying them access to other schools that served White students.

  The human side of this case is that Mendez is the surname of the Mexican American family whose eight-year-old daughter, Sylvia, was refused admission to her neighborhood school for not being White. Her father, Gonzalo Mendez, was a trusted employee of a Japanese American farmer who was forced into an internment camp during World War II. While interned, the Minumutsu family put Mr. Mendez in charge of the farm and had the Mendez family move into their home, in a more desirable neighborhood than where they had been living. When the family went to register the children in their closest school, they were denied and mandated to attend the Mexican School in the low-income neighborhood.

Besides the proximity concerns, there were stark differences beyond the ethnic profile of schools for Mexican students versus those for White students. Mexican Schools were substandard and not close to being like the other schools in every way, from the facilities to the materials, equipment, textbooks, and staffing. Feeling that this was an unjust system for their children, the Mendez and other families filed a suit against the district. US District Court Judge Paul J. McCormick wrote that:

> The equal protection of the laws pertaining to the public school system in California is not provided by furnishing in separate schools the same technical facilities, textbooks and courses of instruction to children of Mexican ancestry that are available to the other public school children regardless of their ancestry. A paramount requisite in the American system of public education is social equality. It must be open to all children by unified school association regardless of lineage.

This California desegregation case was significant in that it would later serve as a precedent for the *Brown* case, which outlawed segregation across the nation.

In addition to the historical legacy of school segregation, the dilemma faced by Dr. Durán requires familiarity with the educational research on tracking. First, let us define *tracking*. Tracking is the practice of grouping students by performance level (or perceptions about performance level) for much or all of their educational experience. Though there are many dimensions to the practice of grouping students, the general consensus of the research is clear: Tracking struggling students into "low academic classes" is educationally unsound and fundamentally inequitable (Oakes, 2005).

Here is a compelling yet counterintuitive example many educators have experienced. Middle or high school students are assessed to determine who is algebra ready. Those deemed not yet ready are placed into a two-year algebra class that slows down the presentation of the material with the intent to help students be more successful. However, in district after district, the evidence shows that when grades and test scores are posted, this group of students consistently has the highest failure rates and lowest test scores in algebra when compared with students who are placed in one-year algebra courses. Tracking students into these easier classes with watered down academic content actually increases failure rates.

Dr. Durán needed a working knowledge of equity-related information from the history of American education and from educational research to be able to accurately see the conditions experienced by the new students in his schools. He was developing equity vision when his eye picked up on the students playing separately on the yard and he wondered about the implications. Without that eye, Dr. Durán may have completely missed the social patterns and never even questioned the existence of systemic practices with severe negative consequences for students.

Leadership Acumen

Take yourself back to a time when you encountered a practice that you absolutely knew was just bad for students and wrong.

- How does that feel?
- What goes through your mind?
- What do you do?

Leadership acumen is an expression of leadership that is astute and measured. When encountering inequitable school systems, leadership acumen provides the restraint required to take meaningful action in a thoughtful manner. Absent leadership acumen, emotions can overtake well-meaning leaders and render them not credible to the very people they need to inspire to think differently.

At first, Dr. Durán was very disturbed at the way his school chose to serve the new students. Then he realized that he was actually disappointed in himself. How did he allow this to unfold? He returned to his office in a very bad mood but thought better of his initial impulse, which was to immediately call in the teachers of the new classes to share his concerns.

However, he realized that the entire staff had also bought into the model because segregating the new students removed them from the worry list of the rest of the staff. The staff at large could rest easier knowing that their colleagues were responding to the needs of the new students and that there was no need for them to change their teaching practices.

So Dr. Durán waited a day and then held a staff meeting. In one form or another, teachers made the case for why the new-student design was advantageous to the new students, the existing students, and to teachers.

Interests versus Positions

A very important skill in dealing with equity-related dilemmas is the ability to dig beneath the words people use and get to their *interests*—that is, the needs, fears, desires, or values that result in those words. More often than not, people speak in terms of *positions*, or what it is they want. Equity leaders who can tell the difference between interests and positions are much better equipped to provide leadership when dilemmas arise.

In this example, the staff expressed only good intentions for students as they provided their rationales for the design of the new-student program. But Dr. Durán knew that they also had other adult interests that they did not verbalize. They were trying to navigate the discomfort among some staff, parents, and community about the demographic shift at the school.

Dr. Durán could not in good conscience allow this segregation practice to continue. But how should he proceed? Recall that the central office was aware of the challenge but left the school on its own to figure it out. He quickly thought about the possibilities:

* E-mailing teachers to direct them to stop their new-student program
* Calling each teacher on the phone and giving them a week to end the programs (with an implied *or else!*)
* Calling a community meeting for new and long-standing parents to discuss the program and explain why he was ending it

Thankfully, Dr. Durán ultimately rejected each of these options. He understood the need to cultivate the staff as a critical equity team in full partnership with him. After some thought, Dr. Durán decided how best to proceed.

Presume Positive Intentions

Presuming positive intentions is a conscious decision on the part of an equity leader. Schools and districts are filled with people who are filled with stories about other people and are often all too eager to share. We know that people behave differently depending on what they believe about those with whom they interact. If we respect others, we behave respectfully and people feel respected. When we think ill of others, people feel it no matter how hard we try to mask it.

It requires discipline and focus for most of us not to fall into the trap of letting unhelpful thoughts creep into our minds. This is difficult for most of us. However, when approaching sensitive equity issues, it is important for leaders to approach teams, students, parents, and community with a pure and open heart—to presume positive intentions to set the necessary tone for a constructive outcome.

After reflecting deeply on his options, Dr. Durán called a staff meeting. He planned to share feedback from the round of class visits he just finished. He knew that the teachers were nervous but very eager to hear his thoughts. Dr. Durán made the conscious decision to believe that as a group, the staff was composed of good-hearted and hard-working educators who truly wanted to serve all their students well. He decided to move forward as if that were 100 percent true.

With notes in hand and a slideshow on the screen, Dr. Durán addressed the group. He was so involved in the content of his presentation that an hour flew by. When he was done, he refocused his eyes on the staff and was perplexed at the look on their faces. Their expressions ranged from anger, to frustration, to upset, to the point of tears. Dr. Durán was a collaborative leader and had a very good relationship with the staff, so their reactions mattered very much to him.

For a minute, he did not know how to proceed. He thought to himself, "I don't know what to say!" He wondered what was going on and what were they thinking, and he very much wished he understood their reaction. Dr. Durán took a breath, turned off the computer, and sat in a chair in front of the group.

When You Get Stumped, Think Aloud

Have you ever been in a situation that was so surprising, confusing, or otherwise emotional that you were at a loss for words? Has anyone ever said anything to you or in your presence that you knew you should respond to, but you were rendered speechless, not knowing how to respond? Here are a few useful tips for such situations.

- When you don't know what to say, just say what you are thinking. Say, "I don't know what to say."
- Then check in with your emotions and say what you are feeling, such as, "I feel very uneasy by this conversation, but I can't explain why just yet. When I am ready, I will come back to discuss this some more."

This strategy gives us time to gain composure and it creates a bit of time and space to determine an appropriate response. Otherwise, in the heat of the moment, a misstep is likely. Hurtful words and behaviors may be forgiven, but they are rarely forgotten.

In the example of Dr. Durán, he was sure he'd made a compelling argument against the new-student program design, but the teachers' expressions told a different story. So he said, "I don't know what to say." Then he asked the group to please clue him in to their thinking by putting words to their reactions. He gave them only one rule—and this is a very important one to include—"Tell me anything you want, just tell me nicely." He explained that if the communication he received was hurtful, he would not be able to truly hear them. So with a smile he said, "No eye-rolling or lip smacking!"

It took them a few moments, but then they started to open up. And once they did, they *really* did! They expressed their feelings about the district and the principal leaving them alone to deal with the challenge of the new students, and they had done the best they knew how to do, and now they were told it was wrong. They had spent time, money, energy, and worry designing their programs. They got staff and parents on board, even when they all had different points of view. Now were they supposed to undo all of that? No, they did not want to undo their programs. Dismantling the new-student classes would impact every class on campus and every teacher.

Try on Someone Else's Shoes

Once we create some time and space to craft a response—a "Twix moment," for commercial watchers—craft that response we must! Where do we start? The most effective and often most underused strategy is simply to demonstrate empathy. To do that, we must truly put ourselves in the shoes of the people we want to understand.

This is much easier said than done, as any parent can testify. Imagine a teenager choosing not to study and failing an important exam. The parent may try to empathize in an effort to understand the child's interests underlying that behavior. The parent's thought process might go something like this: "I was a teenager once. I remember that I had many competing priorities also." This is where the exercise often crashes. "But I would *never* care about anything more than schooling. I *always* wanted to make my parents proud . . ." This ceased to be empathy as soon as the parent imposed a personal value judgment onto the child's behavior.

Here is how Dr. Durán proceeded. First, he validated the teachers' feelings, but not just symbolically. He really put himself in their shoes and openly shared that in the same circumstances, he would feel the same way. He assured them that he did not intentionally put them in a position that would undermine their sense of ownership of their schools. He openly recalled experiences like that when he was a teacher and pledged not to do that to them.

Very often, people's resistance to change initiatives comes from four sources:

1. Limited content knowledge;
2. A lack of sound technical expertise on how to deal with new educational situations;
3. Anxiety about not being able to navigate potential politics; and
4. A sense of loss of some sort (power, respect, prestige, autonomy).

In the example, the staff heard that their only plan was wrong, and they had no Plan B. And they were correct that the district and principal had provided no direction, so they did the best they could with the information they had.

Teachers were also detecting rumblings of clashes between groups with differing perspectives about the demographic transition, which worried them. Finally, they felt their existing instructional plans were effective and they were anxious because they had no experience with any other way to teach.

Fairly quickly, civility between parents representing the new and existing families began to break down as competition for resources began to emerge. Community organizations representing both factions in the city began to have heated discussions about the school in city council and town hall meetings. And students and teachers from the different groups began to exhibit resentment, distancing themselves from one another.

Make Sure You Can Walk in Their New Shoes

If there is one hard rule when leading a change movement of the sort required to disrupt inequitable educational practices, here it is: We must be sure that we ourselves can do whatever we are asking others to do. If the change proposal does not pass this basic test, do not advance the proposal.

Dr. Durán demonstrated that he could not only point out the inequitable practices with the new students, but that he could also design a workable equity plan. This was his equity proposal:

- Cluster five or six new students in a regular grade-level class. Place students in their appropriate grade level.
- During the summer, provide teachers with a summer institute on differentiation strategies so that they can tailor teaching in whole group some of the time and in leveled small group other times.
- Provide teacher teams with staff meeting time for the rest of the year to design short, frequent mastery checks so that they can check on student progress in real time and quickly make adjustments to more strategically meet student needs.
- Invite all students for optional enrichment classes and an expanded-day program for additional accelerating instruction. Encourage parents of struggling students (new *and* continuing) to make sure their children attend.
- Design target classes with creative and engaging ways to preview and review core grade-specific content, using technology tools, project-based instruction, and models or manipulatives.

DID THE STAFF GO ALONG WITH THE PLAN?

With such a straightforward solution, Dr. Durán was confident that the staff would follow his recommendation to move from their segregated support programs to this more integrated accelerating design. Alas, they did not! This is real life. Sometimes, in spite of the most thoughtful facilitation, people just don't easily adopt change initiatives. Most often this is because their personal interests were not satisfied by the proposal. In this situation, teachers came to understand that their current approach was poor and needed to stop, but they did not have confidence that they could convince some parents and all teachers that the clusters were going to work. They articulated several interests:

- Longtime parents might take issue with having "mixed" classes because they feared it would water down expectations for the majority of the students.
- Longtime parents might want new students to participate in intervention programs, where they might be more successful, away from the continuing students.
- New parents might feel that their children were not receiving the degree of support they needed.
- Teachers still might feel they were not able to meet the range of needs in mixed classes.
- Teachers who felt their strength involved working with struggling students might feel that only a small group of teachers at the school had the experience to teach the new students.

Dr. Durán listened to the teachers' feedback on his proposal for a half hour. Then, one teacher asked him point-blank, "Are you directing us to do this? If we don't have a real choice, then please just tell us now and we will figure it out."

Dr. Durán replied, "No, I'm not telling you that you have to implement my solution. I don't want you to implement something you don't support. I *am* saying that we cannot continue with the current design. Let me be clear— *I want you to want to do this.*"

"What?"

"That's right, I want you to *want* to implement heterogeneous classes with strategic differentiation and leveled expanded-day extra support."

Empower with Clear Parameters

People often think that *empowerment* means giving others freedom to do as they wish. This could not be further from the truth when it comes to providing every child with the education they deserve. When equity leaders give people freedom to do as they wish, it is an abdication of the sacred trust to care for all students, especially the most vulnerable. The appropriate method of nurturing an equity team is to empower members by providing clear parameters that ensure that equity considerations are met.

Dr. Durán repeated, "I want you to want to implement the redesign I suggest for the reasons I shared. However, if you choose not to, then propose a better solution. I am open to listening to all suggestions. Here are the criteria. Proposals:

- must give every child the best opportunity to maximize their learning and achievement;
- must be grounded in research and best practice; and
- must adhere to legal requirements."

Dr. Durán empowered the staff to take up the redesign challenge: "I want you to want to try the design I propose because it is a true, right, and just way to support all students. You may suggest alternatives. But please know that in the absence of a better approach, I will ask that we move in this direction for the next school year."

The teachers felt empowered to innovate, and they knew the parameters. Only one teacher proposed an alternative plan that met all the parameters, but it was more difficult to implement, and after one year the teacher joined the school approach the following year.

Teacher feedback about implementation of the new redesign made clear that without proper support, teachers would have difficulty implementing the program, even if they were willing. So Dr. Durán added additional teacher coaching and collaborative planning time. Success was not immediate, but over the next two years, instruction for all students was visibly stronger, and the new student/old student culture was a faint memory in the minds of most.

When Dr. Durán looks back on that chapter in his career, he often asks himself where that came from: "I want you to want to?" *Goodness!* Wherever it came from, it helped get the school through a difficult time without compromising what was right for students and without squashing the adults whose life work it is to serve them.

EQUITY HOOK: I WANT YOU TO WANT TO

SUMMARY

This chapter tells the story of a school where student demographics dramatically shifted when a population of low-income students arrived as a result of gentrification in their home neighborhood. The new students had substantial academic challenges. We describe the challenging and somewhat painful process and growth that one leader, Dr. Durán, experienced in his attempt to disrupt segregation of the new students while maintaining a culture of staff empowerment.

Dr. Durán understood the need to develop an equity team of teachers who were in full partnership with him to move the school forward. He assumed goodwill among the teachers and proceeded to move forward, but he still had resistance. He identified three sources of this resistance.

Dr. Durán's approach was to give staff the option to adopt his plan or to propose their own plan that had to adhere to three parameters:

- The plan must give every child the best opportunity to maximize their learning achievement.
- It must be grounded in research and best practice.
- It must adhere to legal requirements.

His statement was, "I want you to want to implement my equity proposal. But if you don't, propose something better that adheres to the criteria." After being given the opportunity to design an equity plan that met the parameters, the teachers decided to implement Dr. Durán's plan. This chapter described how Dr. Durán set the conditions for the teachers to feel empowered—without compromising the needs of students—fueled by the simple Equity Hook "I want you to want to."

EQUITY CONCEPTS

- *Equity Vision:* This is the state of being able to study a situation and discern whether and how it promotes or suppresses equitable outcomes for students.
- *Leadership Acumen:* This is an expression of leadership that is astute and measured that provides the restraint required to take meaningful action in a thoughtful manner.
- *Interests versus Positions:* This is the ability to dig beneath the words people use and get to their *interests*: that is, their needs, fears, desires, or values that result in those words, rather than accepting statements of strict positions on issues.

EQUITY ACTIONS

- Presume positive intentions. When approaching sensitive equity issues, it is important for the leader to approach the teams, students, parents, and community with a pure and open heart, and to behave as if you know they are doing the same.
- When you get stumped, think aloud. This is a strategy that gives leaders time to gain composure and creates a bit of time and space to compose an

appropriate response when caught off guard. Otherwise, in the heat of the moment, a misstep is likely.

- Say, "I don't know what to say."
- Then say, "I don't feel comfortable at the moment. I need some time to process this. When I arrive at clarity, we will revisit this."

- Try on their shoes. The most effective and often most underused strategy in the midst of conflict is simply to experience and demonstrate empathy.
- Make sure you can walk in their new shoes. We must be sure that *we* ourselves can do whatever we are asking others to do. If the change proposal does not pass this basic test, do not advance the proposal.
- Empower with clear parameters. Equity leaders who give people freedom to do as they wish abdicate their sacred trust to care for all students, especially the most vulnerable. The appropriate method of nurturing an equity team is to empower members by providing clear parameters that ensure that equity considerations are met.

Chapter Six

The Power of Expectations

Equity Hook: Language Is a Window into Belief Systems

Have you ever wondered . . .

- What role belief systems play in school and district practices?
- How to figure out what beliefs serve as the foundation for a school or district?
- Whether there is a way to "decode" conversations to identify the underlying beliefs about students and families accepted as the norm?
- What the relationship is between language and worldview?

Belief systems are the foundation of every decision made in a school system. Yet the beliefs that generated existing practices are not often articulated; rather, they are inside the conscious and not-so-conscious minds of people who are part of the system. Equity leaders like the teacher and administrator in the following example rescued an entire family of children from educational decisions that would have relegated them to second-class citizenship. These leaders understood the practical implications of the Equity Hook, "language is a window into belief systems."

MEET PRECIOUS

Precious Cantor began experiencing trouble in school in kindergarten. By the second grade, it was clear that Precious was distractible, unfocused, and academically behind her peers. Her second-grade teacher, concerned at her lack of progress, requested a student study team meeting (SST) that included key school staff and Precious's mother. At the SST, Mrs. Cantor shared that

Precious's father was in prison and that she was raising Precious and four younger children on her own.

The impact of that information on the team was notable, and the team immediately requested a full assessment for Precious. The results determined that Precious had auditory processing problems and qualified for special education services. She was placed in a resource specialist program (RSP) where a special education teacher or aide "pushed-in" to the general education classroom several days a week, for several hours, to help Precious keep up in class.

Though Precious made some progress, it was slow. Both the general education and special education staff members were frustrated with the rate of her progress, but they reminded themselves of her unfortunate family circumstances and were pleased with any progress at all. Precious participated in the RSP program the entire year, but she fell further and further behind.

IT'S A FAMILY AFFAIR

When Precious began third grade, her little sister Valerie started school. Within the first month of school, the staff recognized her as Precious's sister. As her kindergarten teacher heard more and more about Precious and the Cantor family from other staff, she was able to detect subtle potential problems in Valerie's learning profile. Valerie had a short attention span, liked to move around frequently, became tired in the afternoon, and often forgot to return homework. As a result, the teacher requested that Valerie be assessed for possible learning disabilities.

The district discouraged special education testing for young students, so in the meantime, an SST was held in which the discussion centered on reducing academic pressure on Valerie because of her difficult family situation and her presumed limited abilities. She was given easier class work, and homework was reduced and made optional for her. Additionally, communication with Mrs. Cantor was kept to a minimum so as not to contribute to her already challenging life. By the end of the following year, Valerie was placed in RSP.

When Precious started fourth grade, Larry, a new RSP teacher, and Susie, a new assistant principal, began working at the school. At the first Individualized Education Program (IEP) meeting of the school year, they noted that Precious had met each and every goal set forth in the previous year's IEP, yet she was failing every subject. Upon further examination, they realized that she had met her goals because the goals were written at a first-grade level! They questioned her previous teachers about her lack of progress and were reminded that she was an RSP child and that it was great that she had made some gains.

Uncomfortable with that response, Larry and Susie determined that without a disruption of her current program, the future was bleak for Precious and her sister, who would become just another statistic. "Not on our watch!" was the promise they made to one another on behalf of the Cantor children.

WHAT'S IN A NAME?

Decision-making processes in schools and districts, so often taken for granted, directly impact the lives and future opportunities of students. The practice of labeling students has enormous implications for equity and is associated with long-term life consequences (Avelar La Salle & Johnson, 2016; Becker, 1963; Harry & Klingner, 2006; Olson, 2004).

Our intent is to highlight the need to unravel processes—and especially the assumptions upon which they are founded—in some school and district cultures that result in disproportionately inclusion or exclusion of students in specialized programs. Disproportionate mislabeling and placement for the most vulnerable populations of students very often results in segregating them from their mainstream peers and pushing them further and further from grade-level expectations.

Conversely, disproportionate underlabeling of the same students to high-status educational programs (i.e., Gifted and Talented Education, Advanced Placement, International Baccalaureate, Honors) denies them the opportunity for premium schooling and further perpetuates the underachievement of historically struggling groups. Equity leaders like Larry and Susie have a heightened awareness of and sense of urgency about examining school and district practices.

For example, the intent of special education services is to employ teachers who are specially trained in appropriate instructional techniques that will give students the special learning support they need to be academically successful. In the story of Precious, the somewhat **sassy** RSP teacher and assistant principal asked themselves why she was still receiving RSP services. As they put it, "The point of all this extra (and expensive) help is to support her to meet grade-level expectations, and yet Precious is failing across the board. If failing were the goal, she could do that for free!"

The Liability of Labeling

Labels on students set off a chain of events in schools that either advantage or disadvantage them, with little impact from their own effort, initiative, or ability. For example, nearly 6 million children in the United States between the ages of six and twenty-one receive some category of special education services. However, fewer than 12 percent of those students are diagnosed with significant cognitive disabilities. Instead almost 88 percent are in categories with relatively subjective criteria, such as learning disabilities and emotional disturbance, and almost 90 percent of the children who are diagnosed with "specific learning disabilities" have problems with reading (Olson, 2004).

Equity leaders must draw attention to the categories that demonstrate the overrepresentation or underrepresentation of different groups. If, for example, students in special education programs overwhelmingly met with academic success, as is the intention, we would all welcome the disproportionate placement patterns of poor and minority students. However, the data on achievement of special education students is dismal, particularly for minority and low-income students. These conditions should cause major equity concerns and action.

Most special education students' experiences include:

- lower levels of academic achievement;
- very low graduation rates;
- a dropout rate about twice the rate of students in general education programs;
- lower performance on state proficiency exams compared with general education peers; and
- higher rates of suspension and expulsion (Ford, 2016).

With such grim results, it is morally imperative for equity leaders to be hypervigilant about processes that label students and ensure that discussions center around the service needs of students, rather than a program that is determined by a label. More than that, equity leaders must peel back the wallpaper to determine the systemic root of the disproportionate labeling. In other words, since every system is perfectly designed to get the results it gets, then what is the system that results in disproportionate labeling?

The Power of Expectations

Great debate exists regarding how appropriate it is to expect all students to reach grade-level proficiency. Certainly, requiring that youngsters with severe cognitively delays take a grade-level exam is unreasonable. However, the majority of students receiving special education services are assessed as intellectually within typical ranges.

These students are in the programs either because of a specific, diagnosed learning challenge or, more often, because they are struggling academically—most often with reading—with no specific identifiable cause. For poor and minority students, this is often because early schooling did not meet their specific needs due to poor program design, unsound grouping practices, less-than-ideal first instruction, insufficient support, or simply low expectations—

that amorphous educational glass ceiling. Excluding these students from grade-level rigor seals their dismal academic fate.

In the story of Precious, lowered expectations were turned on their head. Here is how. Larry spoke to Mrs. Cantor to better understand Precious's academic history. Mrs. Cantor explained that, among other things, her husband's family was affiliated with gangs and he was currently incarcerated. Precious was the eldest of five children. During the conversation, Mrs. Cantor showed the teacher a letter that her husband sent her that had amazing artwork bordering it.

The teacher admired the artwork and listened to Mrs. Cantor as she shared that Precious had received two very positive gifts from her father: an eye for art and the ability to sing. The next day, the teacher asked Precious to demonstrate some of her talents, and she was in fact a gifted artist and an amazing vocalist. Larry and Susie convened an IEP meeting to purposefully encourage art and singing to develop Precious's confidence and self-esteem, and rewrote her academic goals to match grade-level expectations.

The overriding question for them was: What conditions would be necessary for Precious to reach grade level in two years?

The first issue discussed was whether it was reasonable to expect Precious to ever reach grade level as a special education student. Larry and Susie reminded the team that to qualify for RSP, Precious was assessed to have average cognitive ability, and they posed the question again: "What conditions would be necessary for Precious to reach grade level in two years?"

The next issue discussed was the difficulty of Precious's home situation and its likely negative impact on the child's ability to focus. In response, Larry and Susie shared samples of the incredibly intricate artwork Precious had produced, obviously requiring an immense degree of focus and persistence, and then they repeated the question: "What conditions would be necessary for Precious to reach grade level in two years?"

The general education teacher stated that she was not opposed to helping Precious more, but in light of the large class size, she felt it impossible to devote the necessary amount of attention to any one child. Susie responded by appreciating the teacher's willingness to be supportive and acknowledged the challenges of meeting the diverse needs of an entire classroom of children, and then restated the question, clearly and deliberately: What conditions would be necessary for Precious to reach grade level in two years?

The IEP meeting continued this way for about ninety minutes, until the general education teacher finally stopped and said, "You really and truly believe that if we got the conditions right that Precious could actually be on grade level before she leaves our school?" Larry and Susie nodded. After a moment of collective silence, the team took a big breath and set out to design a plan built on the premise that Precious would be on grade level by the end of the fifth grade. This experience forever altered how IEP meetings were run for every student who followed.

Specific action steps will follow later in the chapter, but the end of this true story is that Precious made rapid gains during her fourth- and fifth-grade years, actually meeting minimum grade-level expectations in all subjects and meeting the criteria to exit from RSP prior to entering middle school. Having been given multiple opportunities to develop and share her artistic and vocal abilities, she came to be seen as something of a child prodigy in the school and around the community, winning art competitions and regularly performing before amazed audiences. Precious performed an original song at her fifth-grade promotion ceremony, and there was not a dry eye in the audience as she sang: fully dressed as Cyndi Lauper with florescent ponytail holders and fingerless gloves—fully confident—and on grade level.

As an aside, Precious's remarkable achievement caused the RSP teacher to also reassess her sister Valerie. While the current general education teacher continued to feel that Valerie required major program modifications to keep up, the school psychologist's assessments determined that Valerie was within normal ranges in all areas.

Susie decided that Valerie would benefit from a new experience. She changed Valerie's class and assigned her to a teacher who had been on Precious's IEP team. The new teacher soon reported that while Valerie did not have the same creative talents as her sister, she was "just as sharp as her sister," and was doing well with the unmodified grade-level curriculum, receiving the same degree of support that many other students required. By the end of that school year, Valerie too met the criteria to transition out of RSP.

It is interesting to note that most university students studying to be teachers or school administrators are knowledgeable and sensitive to the notion that adults' expectations of students have a powerful effect on their own behavior, which ultimately translates into an effect on student behavior and achievement. While they are taking college courses, these educators-in-training readily accept the idea that adult expectations for students manifest themselves in subtle and not-so-subtle cues. Over time, student behavior and performance respond to those cues and ultimately expectations—either positive or negative—are confirmed. These educators vow to never fall into that trap.

Once on the job, however, many educators react defensively to the same notion, arguing that educators are not generally biased and that students are primarily—if not exclusively—responsible for their own performance. The idea that they may be participants in a system where expectations are different not only for individual students, but also for entire demographic groups (i.e., social class, race, gender) can be too personal to process.

Spillover Effect

For Precious and her siblings, the power of the expectations held for the children was the single most significant variable in their academic trajectory. At first, well-meaning adults had sincere compassion for the children's difficult home situation. They had a perception of what it must be like to have a father in jail and be part of a home in which a single parent was raising five young children. Based on that perception, the adults at the school made decisions about how best to help the children that actually magnified their learning challenges. In the case of Precious, her IEP goals were written several grade levels below her grade level, and her failures were celebrated.

For her sister Valerie, the spillover effect resulted in preemptive modifications to her program designed to simplify what might *potentially* become too complicated for her. As a result, her homework demands were reduced, her class work was simplified, expectations that she would develop age-appropriate study skills were eliminated, and the decision was made to avoid communication about her deficits with her mother.

Since the district discouraged identifying young children for special education, the school used alternate methods to identify Valerie as learning disabled. These methods were heavily reliant on subjective teacher rating sheets. The prevailing beliefs about Precious and the Cantor family's circumstances were so strong that they influenced even the assessment process that was perceived as objective.

In fact, so-called objective assessments used for program identification are often subjective. Even in an assessment context, human judgment and interpretation can lead to very different decisions and outcomes for students. The difficulty is that belief systems and attitudes about individuals and groups are often subconscious and also taboo. So, very often we avoid fully explaining the reasoning behind our recommendations for students. Therefore, decisions based on differential expectations go largely unnoticed and are usually uncontested, except by equity leaders like Larry and Susie.

While the story of the Cantor children ended favorably, it almost did not. All too often the ending is far from happy for entire groups of students. What conditions propelled Precious from severe academic deficiency to grade-level achievement? The success was the result of the collaborative equity leadership of the RSP teacher and the assistant principal, who disrupted an inequitable labeling process built on inaccurate, biased, and dangerous assumptions.

Hidden Belief System Code

If you want to know what people's beliefs are about students, listen carefully for hidden language clues. The language adults use when discussing students provides keen insight into their underlying assumptions, beliefs, and expectations about children. When the assumptions, beliefs, and expectations become institutional norms, entire school systems begin to operate under those beliefs.

When the assumptions, beliefs, and expectations are inaccurate, this phenomenon can result in dire consequences for entire groups of students. A kind of educational apartheid evolves in schools whereby students such as Precious are sorted into permanent categories.

In one extremely disturbing example, students in one school who moved in ways typically associated with African American youth were described by adults as exhibiting "strolling." Strolling is perceived to be aggressive behavior by teachers, and worthy of harsh discipline. Other students who engaged in rule-breaking behavior not perceived as strolling were not harshly punished (Neal, McCray, Webb-Johnson, & Bridgest, 2003). They argue in compelling language that being poor in and of itself may not cause students to be academically underdeveloped; what does is how the culture and the organization of the school situates minority youth as academically and behaviorally deficient and places them at risk.

In the story of Precious, belief systems expressed by language played a significant role in her educational plan. At the time her first teacher noticed some learning problems in class, when the first meetings were held, and when her mother was interviewed, the school team used language when describing Precious that was simply inaccurate. This went unchallenged until the new RSP teacher and assistant principal arrived and began to peel off the wallpaper.

Textbox 6.1 highlights language samples from the IEP meetings, which were collected and analyzed by Susie. She subsequently used these data to bring to light the underlying implied—yet operating—assumptions about Precious. These assumptions, which later proved to be erroneous, resulted in educational decisions that had clearly harmed Precious's academic progress.

Whether the individuals involved intended it or not, the result of this language was the acceptance of a perceived reality about the child's academic capacity that led to institutional acceptance and the normalization of low expectations. This became the rationale for decisions that actually harmed Precious.

TEXTBOX 6.1. LANGUAGE SAMPLES COLLECTED BY THE NEW ASSISTANT PRINCIPAL

She has lower ability.
She is working to her *potential*.

She is doing the best she can [though she is failing].
She is trying to keep up with the *brighter* students.
All we can ask is that she *try her best*.
Let's give her goals that she *can actually meet.*
She's an *intervention student* so . . .
For an *RSP student*, she . . .
She is *learning disabled.*

While this language may seem benign to some, it resulted in a shared perception about Precious that was limiting and inaccurate. Language has the power to evolve into an institutional reality that becomes the basis for decisions and actions that affect the long-term lives of students in profound ways.

Figure 6.1 demonstrates how language can be interpreted in ways that create hurtful impressions about students. Table 6.1 lists the language samples used by the team and highlights the possible corresponding interpretations and conclusions about Precious.

Even if the speakers do not *intend* to communicate lesser expectations, listeners may receive that message. This issue is not limited to special education but is linked to and reflects the institutional culture of school and affects how students are perceived. The language used can also result in positive outcomes, such as those descriptions used for students who are in perceived high-status programs.

Sadly, history and research teach us that beliefs exist not only for individual students like Precious, but also for different populations of students. These beliefs result in high-stakes educational decisions that affect students for life. Using the Cantor family as an example, let us trace how language is a secret code for beliefs that define a student's educational trajectory. Figure

Figure 6.1. Language Interpretation Process

Table 6.1. Language Samples and Possible Interpretations

Language	Possible Interpretations
• She has lower ability. • She is trying to keep up with the *brighter* students. • All we can ask is that she *try her best.*	She was just not born as smart as other students and therefore will never be able to do as well as her classmates. Because of her low-income background she is intellectually underdeveloped.
• She is doing the best she can. • She is working to her *potential.*	There is a fixed, predetermined, and inborn limit to every person's intelligence. We, as professionals, are able to determine that point for students. There is no sense trying to insist that Precious perform beyond this point because it is simply not possible.
• She's an intervention student. • She is an RSP student.	The programs and services Precious receives define her as a student and as a person. She is qualitatively different from other students and just not as good a student.
• But she is learning disabled.	She is not able to learn as well as other students. Her academic deficits are inevitable and we are powerless to change that.
• Let's give her goals that she *can actually meet.*	She obviously cannot reach high levels of academic achievement, and we do not want to be held accountable for her lack of success. Her failure will make the school look bad and make the adults feel terrible. Therefore, let's set lower goals so that we can document that Precious has at least met the legal requirements that she met IEP goals, and maybe she and the adults will feel better about themselves.

6.2 illustrates what happened when staff members were asked how they were specifically addressing Precious's needs.

The RSP teacher and aide answered in like fashion, noting that they had not reviewed her IEP for a while, but that Precious had trouble learning.

Equity leaders must listen carefully to the language used when discussing individual students and groups of students to find clues to the underlying beliefs that become institutional systems—systems that have long since stopped being questioned and are normalized. Larry and Susie took decisive steps to disrupt the system in their school that was limiting the opportunities of the Cantor children and so many others like them.

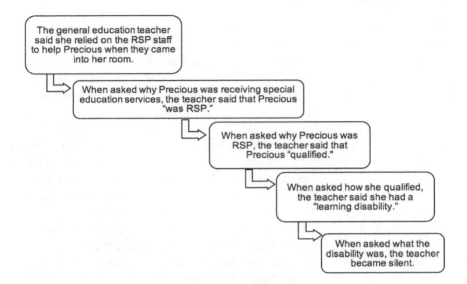

Figure 6.2.   Description of Imprecise Support for Precious

Become Fluent in Equity Language

Equity language refers to discourse that reflects the expectation that every student, highlighting those representing historically struggling groups, is entitled to the best education regardless of ZIP code. Equity leaders must be conscious of the language used by others as well as the language we use ourselves when discussing students. This takes practice.

Often, we are so accustomed to hearing the language of inequity that it has become normalized and we do not even notice it. One helpful way to develop fluency in equity language is to replicate the process Susie applied.

- Sit in a setting where people are discussing students.
- Transcribe as much of the language possible.
- Place the language snippets into the left column of a table modeled after table 6.1 with the heading "Language."
- For each language snippet, imagine the implied subtext or possible connotation, and write that into a second column labeled "Possible Interpretations." This process is best done with a trusted colleague or friend, rather than independently, so that the normalization has the best chance of being disrupted.

Use Data-Derived Language

The first element of Precious's revised educational plan was to gain clarity on her specific learning profile and how it negatively affected her learning. Then the team committed to using accurate language to represent her profile. In fact, the original multidisciplinary team conduced a comprehensive assessment process to determine that Precious had specific auditory processing deficits. This is like dyslexia of the ears: Her hearing is perfect, but her brain jumbles the language she hears, making it difficult for her to fully comprehend language. This especially affects literacy development. It also manifests itself in a lack of focus or attention, as the strain of trying to understand the massive language input she receives in school becomes fatiguing. This identification was used to qualify her to participate in RSP but was never again highlighted. The generic language of *special education* or *RSP* was the focus until Larry and Susie arrived. Labeling a student simply as RSP or special education is not informative or helpful in developing an acceleration plan.

Sadly, RSP and special education labels often erroneously connote "less intelligent." Therefore, the first part of the plan was to ensure that everyone involved with Precious discussed her in light of her auditory processing deficits, which describes her specific, assessed processing weakness. All subsequent plan components stemmed from that premise.

Further, Susie established a norm that the team would use language accurately when discussing Precious and created the expectation to challenge any language that stated or implied anything that was beyond the determination of the assessment data (i.e., intelligence, potential, ability, etc.). The focus of discussion would be on her present performance levels and ways to get her to grade level, acknowledging her learning profile.

Build Need-Based Support Models

Schools and districts are complex systems with myriad responsibilities. An inherent conflict exists between the requirements of running an efficient institution and the needs of individuals or groups of students within the system. In the case of services for struggling students, schools or districts often create a model that is intended to serve all students most efficiently.

Using a schoolwide approach is popular because it is efficient, easier to plan, simpler to budget, and generally more straightforward than the alternative, which is to look specifically at each student and design a plan that responds to the identified learning profile and targets accelerated academic achievement. In the case of Precious, Susie and Larry asked the original IEP team, how the push-in model was decided for her. They responded that it was the schoolwide RSP model. When asked how that model specifically addressed Precious's auditory processing deficits and accelerated progress toward grade-level proficiency, the room went silent.

The second element of Precious's revised educational plan was to build her service model based on her needs. After reviewing her performance and observational data, the team determined that Precious had the best chance of accelerating her academic level if she received instruction in grade-level core curriculum, with support targeting her auditory processing issues.

The plan for Precious included push-in, pull-out, co-teaching, extended day, and specific instructional and self-help strategies. She received support through the use of graphic organizers to supplement verbal input. She was taught to create symbols and pictures to help her conceptualize linguistically complex concepts and she was taught to use an agenda with checklists to help herself keep track of instructions, assignments, and homework. As a result of attention to the details of her plan, Precious made significant academic gains within two months of implementation of the plan.

Establish and Monitor Aggressive Student Outcome Goals

A third element of Precious's plan was to clearly state, verbally and in writing, that the goal was for Precious to reach grade level in two years. Rather than writing oversimplified goals that were within her immediate reach, the school derived quarterly goals by benchmarking backward from fifth-grade standards, assuming accelerated learning would take place beginning in fourth grade. This acceleration was required for Precious to close the gap between her present level of performance and grade-level achievement by the end of the following school year, and the plan was built so that the necessary conditions would exist for that to occur.

Susie closely monitored the weekly and quarterly achievement data to assess Precious's progress and made recommendations for plan refinements if the pace of acceleration was not acceptable. She also collected data on the implementation of the plan by visiting both the general education classroom and the pull-out room frequently, observing the teacher collaboration sessions, and shadowing Precious during different points in her school day. These data helped Susie ensure that the high expectations set for Precious were being honored in daily practice.

The data also helped Susie determine that Valerie's first teacher held beliefs about the child that were helping to perpetuate her learning struggles rather than advancing her learning. Recognizing that changing the teacher's mind-set would take more time than Valerie had, Susie made the decision to move Valerie to another teacher who exhibited very high expectations for every student. This change proved to be pivotal in Valerie's acceleration and ultimate exit from the RSP program.

Also important are the expectations that parents have for their children and that students have for themselves. While schools cannot control the incoming belief systems of parents and students, experience has taught us that schools can have a powerful influence on them. Schools that develop a culture of high expectations and make decisions based on those expectations tend to have students who feel more empowered to achieve and parents who expect their children to be academically successful.

Conversely, schools filled with excuses for why students are not achieving—blaming children; family circumstances; or cultural, racial, or income variables for underachievement—tend to have students who accept their academic levels as inevitable and parents who appear complacent about their children's schooling.

Ultimately, we must collectively acknowledge that we all hold beliefs and expectations about people. It is part of being human. However, real educational harm is done that affects students for the rest of their lives when we are not reflective and when we make the decisions based on those beliefs.

ONE MORE THING

The footnote to this story is that when Precious moved up to middle school, her little brother Gabriel started kindergarten. Since Precious's and Valerie's stories were well-known sources of school pride by this time, Gabriel's arrival was much anticipated. After a month of school, his teacher described him as energetic, enthusiastic, and excited to learn. A "typical little boy," Gabriel was sometimes scattered and forgetful—just part of his charm—and another great Cantor child. No referral was ever made for him.

EQUITY HOOK: LANGUAGE IS A
WINDOW INTO BELIEF SYSTEMS

SUMMARY

This chapter focuses on the role of language, belief systems, and assumptions and their incredible impact on how decisions are made about students in our schools. This example is about students who receive special education services, but similar conditions prevail throughout schools and districts with other vulnerable students in other programs as well as in general education.

The story of Precious sheds light on how decision making based on low expectations and labeling limits students' opportunity to learn. It also demonstrates how beliefs about some students are generalized to others, without evidence to substantiate such comparisons.

Two equity leaders came to the school, a vice principal and a special education teacher. They changed the school culture and interrupted the low expectations for Precious and her sister. They challenged the status quo and used the language of equity to develop an aggressive equity action plan that replaced erroneous assumptions about Precious's capability. They analyzed the language used in the school culture for hidden clues that provided them with insights about underlying expectations, assumptions, and beliefs about students.

The overriding question for the advocates was, "What conditions would be necessary for Precious to reach grade level in two years?" This question was a game changer. The story of the Cantor children is a true story. It describes the possibilities when equity advocates and others have the will to disrupt educational inequities and to make equity action a priority.

EQUITY CONCEPTS

- *The Liability of Labeling:* This is the idea that labels on students set off a chain of events in schools that either advantage or disadvantage them, with little impact from their own effort, initiative, or ability.
- *The Power of Expectations:* This is the notion that adult expectations of students are different not only for individual students, but also for entire demographic groups, and that this results in life-changing decisions made for students.
- *Spillover Effect:* This is the phenomenon in which impressions held about an individual are dangerously generalized to others near or like them (family, friends, or others in the demographic group they represent).
- *Hidden Belief System Code:* The language adults use when discussing students provides keen insight into underlying assumptions, beliefs, and expectations about children. When the assumptions, beliefs, and expectations become institutional norms, entire school systems begin to operate under those beliefs.

EQUITY ACTIONS

- Become fluent in equity language. Equity language refers to discourse that reflects the expectation that every student, highlighting those representing historically struggling groups, is entitled to the best education available, no matter their ZIP code, as well as the support they need to attain grade-level proficiency. Equity leaders must be conscious of the language used by others as well as the language we use ourselves when discussing students.

- Use data-derived language. Use language accurately when discussing students and equity issues, and make it the expectation to challenge any language that states or implies anything that is beyond the determination of objective data (i.e., intelligence, potential, ability, etc.).
- Build need-based support models. Look specifically at each student and design a plan that responds to the identified, data-defined profile to accelerated academic achievement. Do not establish a support model and expect all students to be equally served by it.
- Establish and monitor aggressive student outcome goals. Never plan for modest, incremental growth. Instead, establish aggressive goals that will close achievement gaps in a fixed time period, backward-map actions, and use frequent data monitoring to check for progress or make plan adjustments.

Chapter Seven

Setting the Conditions for Building Collective Equity Muscle

Equity Hook: A Star Does Not a Constellation Make

Have you ever wondered . . .

- What are the implication of individual successes to educational equity?
- The best way to set conditions for equity work to have the best chance of long-term success?
- If there is ever a time when it is appropriate to take immediate action as an individual to disrupt inequities in school systems?

The quest to ensure educational equity for every child attracts all types of personalities. Often, individuals with an equity heart become the standout exemplars of exceptional practice that everyone else points to as equity models. This was the situation for Roy, an administrator new to a school district. Beaming with pride, the district touted many exceptional examples of equity in action. This chapter demonstrates how the existence of individual bright spots is a clear sign of a district in need of attending to equity issues because a star does not a constellation make!

Native Unified School District is a midsized rural district of twenty K–8 schools, half on one side of the tracks and half on the other side—literally. Train tracks separated the higher-income neighborhood from the lower-income area, and each side had its own set of schools. The higher-income schools boasted superior student outcomes on every measure, with the opposite outcome true for the other schools. The achievement of the wealthier schools was so high that the overall district numbers were well above county averages. As a result, the district received considerable acclaim for its results, which was quite pleasing to parents, community, board members, and real estate agents!

Roy was hired as chief academic officer after a search for a leader who could take the district to the next level. Following the advice of his predecessor, he took time to get to know and appreciate the district before launching any new initiatives. As an equity leader, Roy was attracted to the district because of the have/have-not problem, which he felt compelled to help solve.

The district had done some amazing things, among them sustained professional learning for teachers, implementation of a highly successful English language development program (ELD), and a focus on the arts and writing during an era when most districts were solely concerned with basic skills.

"You must spend time at Lake Vista School," he was told. "The way they integrate the arts is amazing!" Sure enough, a visit to that school confirmed that it was amazing at the arts, offering students a masterfully enriched program. "Did you see how Mountain Middle School does writing?" That school's writing samples posted in the district office display boards were impressive by any standard. "Cactus School can take any English learner and help them reach English proficiency before they leave elementary school. Its ELD program is magical." Sure enough, watching the program in action was breathtaking, honoring the students' primary language and culture while skillfully helping them develop formal academic English competence.

As part of his acclimation process, Roy visited every school in the district. He asked each principal to take him through some team collaboration sessions. The district had invested heavily in providing schools with release time for grade-level or course teams of teachers to get together to review assessment data and collaborate on unit or lesson plans. He was thoroughly impressed by the professionalism and depth of reflection of the teams he observed. He also asked principals to take him through classrooms, where he saw some of the most powerful teaching and learning of his educational career.

After several months of this process, Roy was overwhelmed by all the positive information he had gleaned, concluding that this district was truly a "beacon of light" in the county. This was the label that a former superintendent applied many decades earlier, and it continued to be used in local newspaper articles and in board campaigns. A conscientious leader at his core, Roy reflected hard on what would be helpful to share with the superintendent and the board, and how he could add value to his new work home.

As he reviewed his notes from his many visits, conversations, and data reviews, he sat back in his seat and took stock. It was absolutely true that there were exceptional examples of schools, administrators, programs, grade-level and course teams, and teachers across the district—the best he had ever encountered. Then Roy slowed his thinking down. This is a skill that equity leaders must practice:

- Stop
- Slow down
- Think

Roy had an overall sense that the district was strong, but he remembered reviewing reports while was preparing for his interview that indicated that schools on different sides of town had very different profiles. That point was almost lost as the bright spots became the overwhelming focus. He realized that he would need to keep a close eye on his Equity True North to position himself to promote systemic equity because the district culture was one that valued individual successes.

Roy convened the principals for a "Skull Session," a collaborative meeting dedicated to spending quality time thinking through a topic of interest. He asked them to come together to help him better understand the district. He shared his positive impressions of the district and listened to the principals confirm his observations. He reviewed the overall district data and celebrated the district's standing in the county. He congratulated the principals on their efforts.

Then he went for it: He asked them to discuss the "sides of the tracks" issue. After a few quiet moments, the principals began to default to the best examples they had at their schools: star programs, star teams, star teachers, star strategies. Almost protective of their new leader, the principals did all they could to give Roy as many shining examples of excellence as they could. It was then that clarity came.

WHAT IS THE ROADBLOCK TO ADVANCING EQUITY HERE?

Sooner or later, all equity-centered leaders will arrive at one hard, cold realization: The true, right, and just work that needs to be done for our most vulnerable students cannot be done by a single equity leader alone. Equity leaders must make it a priority to cultivate a culture of equity among adults (Lindsey, et al., 2008).

Adults whose charge it is to provide equitable schooling to students must themselves work in equity-promoting adult systems. Roy realized that the district culture rewarded individual accomplishment and simply did not address long-standing disparities. Roy thanked the principals profusely for their enthusiastic accounting of the bright spots in the district, and then he decided to take a calculated risk for the sake of his Equity True North.

He asked if they would accept some pointed questions "in the name of equity." Cautiously, they agreed. Then he asked:

- Are *all* our schools equally excellent?

- Are *all* our programs equally brilliant?
- On all your teams, is everyone a shining example of teamwork and collaboration?
- Is every single one of our teachers a shining star?
- Are each of you . . . ?

Then in a moment of sheer inspiration, Roy quietly said, "A star does not a constellation make."

Equity Culture

Organizational culture refers to an entity's identity as perceived by the adults who constitute that system. *Equity culture* refers to an organizational identity defined by the widespread shared values and common behaviors associated with championing equitable outcomes for all students. This requires that systems encourage and reward equity—the belief that under the right conditions, every part of a system is uplifted and disparities between parts of a system are reduced.

Reform movements come and go. Been there, done that; this too shall pass. However, successful equity efforts that stand the test of time have one thing in common: They cultivate a deeply held equity culture that defines them for years and years past their initial equity launch. The equity ideal characterizes not only conditions crafted for students, but also equitable systemic conditions for the adults devoted to promoting equitable outcomes for students. This requires leaders to assess every part of a school or district to determine whether the system is grounded in the drive to disrupt inequities wherever they occur. Educators who find themselves in inequitable systems are stifled. Their impact is curtailed.

Adult practices that are *not* aligned with an equity culture include:

- teacher team settings where only loudest or most politically charged voices are heard;
- less-effective educators placed in schools with the most vulnerable students and the least advocacy;
- site administrator meetings where district administrators consistently favor some schools over others in their remarks;
- professional learning designs at a school or district that exclude opportunities for elective, physical education, special education, or other specialty teachers to improve their practice;
- districts in which it is accepted that some schools are simply better than others; and
- guidance departments where it is assumed that the stronger counselors will take on the work that less impactful counselors are unable to do.

All of these are examples of conditions adults encounter that limit the potential power of the system to drive toward equitable student outcomes.

BACK TO THE CONSTELLATION

A star does not a constellation make. The air went out of the room. Roy continued, "For us to fulfill our moral imperative to provide *every* child with the excellent education in the way they deserve, we must not be satisfied until every part of our district is exceptional. Think about this. We should actually be saddened, if not angry, that we have stars dotting our district!"

He explained that identifying stars means that others are something lesser: "I'm not saying that we should dull our bright spots simply so they do not outshine the rest. Do not misunderstand. I am saying that we should work each and every day so that everyone—every adult, every team, every department—is shining brilliantly. Only then will every child get every opportunity to which they are entitled. Only then will we have a true equity culture."

Collective Equity Muscle

Collective equity muscle (Johnson & Avelar La Salle, 2010) refers to the magnified power of equity-centered leadership when an equity culture becomes the norm. Elaborating on the constellation metaphor, Roy asked the principals to appreciate that the difference between a few shining stars and a constellation is more than simply a matter of quantity or the degree of light: "Constellations create possibilities that individual stars cannot."

For decades, individual leaders have developed the skill and found the will to address systemic inequities in schools and districts. And still, not enough examples exist of true, sustained turnaround in which demographics ceased to determine educational destiny. Here is one major reason why: While completely doable, the work of disrupting legacy issues of educational inequity is just too complex for any individual or small group to achieve. It is even too much for many individuals working independently. Collective equity muscle exists when mission-aligned people are committed to Equity True North in all its manifestations across a school system.

The principals were quiet. Roy ended the session by explaining that the energy and impact of a constellation is many times greater than that of the aggregate of individually shining stars. He ended with an unexpected challenge. He asked the principals to accept the responsibility of encouraging *all* parts of the district and *all* parts of their schools to excel: "From today forward, it will become unacceptable for us to tout the individual bright spots across the district, because this is a fundamental marker of a lack of equity."

Changing long-standing patterns takes a great deal of commitment to equity, the courage to call out inequities that have become the norm, and the strength to hold school systems to a higher standard.

Roy went back to his office, phoned some trusted equity-centered colleagues from his previous districts for support (and to be inspired by their collective equity muscle), and crafted a plan of action to decrease the disparities across the district as they expressed themselves in every form, for both adults and students. Roy honored the maxim that before an equity plan can be implemented, the conditions for equity work must be set.

Roy recognized that the leadership challenge is to balance the urgency for immediate change with the patience to do it in a way that will take root for the long term—and to have the wisdom to know the difference. This example will describe a set of action steps that create the positive conditions necessary for equity work to take root. Notice that the steps described in this chapter precede any action plan implementation. In other words, we should not rush to implement anything without thoroughly preparing.

Take an Equity Inventory

The first step in creating the conditions for powerful equity work to take root is to take stock of the present equity realities by taking an *equity inventory*. The easiest way to do this is to identify the stars and then contrast them with the non-stars. Table 7.1 demonstrates the line of questioning leaders can take based on their roles.

Roy decided to start the constellation-building work with his district office team. He asked department heads to run through this line of questioning related to the schools. Which are the star schools? What makes them stars? By default, the rest are not stars. That is not acceptable as part of an equity culture.

The team charted two columns: star and non-star schools. As this unfolded, the team realized that the grouping was more nuanced than that. Team members debated the characteristics that made the star schools more effective than the others and realized that there were shades of difference between schools in each column.

For example, the schools on the "right" side of the tracks tended to be in the star column for higher achievement. However, the team discussed how much they could legitimately attribute their achievement to the value added by the school program, since the students in those schools had so many out-of-school resources that other schools did not have.

So the team decided to focus on how vulnerable students achieved in all the schools, on both sides of the tracks, rather than to identify stars by bright-spot programs or overall achievement. This criterion provided an entirely different color to the discussion. High-performing schools with large

Table 7.1.   Taking Equity Inventory

Role	Line of Questioning to Inventory Equity Status	
	Star Examples	*Non-Star Inequities* *Under what conditions . . .*
Teacher	• Who are my star students?	. . . can my other students excel?
	• Who are my star (most collaborative) table groups?	. . . can the rest of my table groups be strong?
Site Administrator	• Who are my star teachers?	. . . can the rest of my teachers be highly effective?
	• Which are my star grade-level or course teacher teams?	. . . can the other teams be as energized?
	• Which are my star front office staff members?	. . . can everyone who greets parents be welcoming and responsive?
District Office Administrator	• Who are the star principals?	. . . can the other principals be as effective at promoting equitable outcomes for students?
		. . . or the equity agenda of the district?
	• Which are the star central office departments?	. . . can the rest of the departments be as equipped to impact the department?
	• Which are the star schools?	. . . can the rest of the schools produce equitable outcomes for most vulnerable students?

achievement gaps for their smaller groups of students in poverty, for example, were placed in the non-star group. And few schools in the lower-income neighborhoods became stars because of the aggressive achievement gains they had made over the past four years, surpassing the achievement of similar students in the wealthier areas and approaching the average achievement across the district.

With this refined equity criteria for the schools, Roy guided them toward their next action step. In Roy's case, the more the team discussed the schools, the fewer schools landed in the star column and the more schools were moved to the non-star column. Thinking this way can become overwhelming because the process indicates that there may be much more need for equity improvement than previously presumed. The next action step is the antidote to that feeling of overwhelm, which can be paralyzing.

Create an Equity Map

Roy facilitated the work of the district office team to create an equity map. An *equity map* is a graphic that tiers units based on an agreed-upon set of criteria. In this example, the unit is the schools and the criterion is achievement levels of the most vulnerable students. Figure 7.1 represents the first draft of the equity map produced by the team. The schools are placed on the map on a continuum of four tiers depending on their need for support in making improvements on achievement for vulnerable students.

Sometimes we can assess the needs to be so great that every unit ends up in tier 4. Here is a tip: The more units that land in the top tier, the more slowly the organization will move toward equity. Simply put, the more we take on as an emergency, the more diluted the support will become and the less aggressive gains will be. Creating an equity map in the shape of a pyramid forces the notion that the units (schools, in this example) at the top—those in need of intensive support—must be fewer than those at the bottom.

The proportions are key. Sometimes when faced with equity issues, it feels like an inverted pyramid, with the point at the bottom and the widest area at the top, and everything requiring intensive support. While this may be true, this stance is not helpful. It leads to feelings of overwhelm and risks burnout and leadership paralysis at a time when clarity and action are most

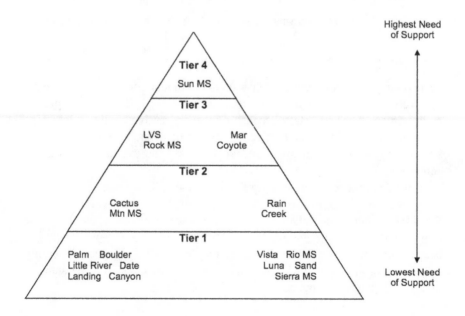

Figure 7.1.   Equity Map for Native School District

required. In such cases, add refining criteria to force finer distinctions among the units. Trust that even among a heap of troubling issues, some are more egregious than others; this will lead to the ability to spread units more proportionally across a pyramid-shaped equity map.

Roy led the district office through deep discussion from the point of view of each department to make connections between how the schools were faring in each of their responsibility areas and their achievement with vulnerable students. For instance, the director of special education noted that schools toward the top tiers had greater difficulty implementing the district design for students with disabilities. The director of student services noted that the schools at the lower tiers had embraced training on restorative practices for student discipline much more deeply than the other schools.

This process of triangulation is important because it adds criteria to the tier placement process and sometimes results in the movement of units up or down based on additional considerations. *Triangulation* is the process of confirming impressions based on multiple sources of data in order to add confidence to those impressions. It also adds voices to the process that might otherwise not be engaged. This buy-in at the outset pays off in constellation dividends as the equity actions proceed.

One final reminder on equity maps is that you can tier any unit in the school system. Recall the line of questioning described in table 7.1. Teachers can tier students or table groups on specific criteria of interest. Principals can tier grade-level teacher teams or special programs at their sites. District office staff can tier schools, departments, or major initiatives. Remember that the goal is not to "grade" anyone or anything. It is not a declaration of effectiveness. Rather, it is a process to ascertain who needs more or different support to arrive at the desired equitable outcome for all parts of the system.

Define Equitable Outcomes

The next step in setting the conditions for equity work is to pause at this point and answer the following question: What equity outcome(s) do we want to see that are not currently part of our reality? In other words, how will you know success when you get there? This seemingly simple exercise is in fact not so easy. As one experienced superintendent shared with his mentee, who was struggling to define equity success, "Sometimes we overeducate ourselves right out of common sense and clear thinking! What do you want your equity reality to be—in plain language?"

For Native School District, the general answer was:

- No difference will exist between the achievement of the target students compared with other students. (This is the ultimate equity point.)

- No difference will exist between the achievement of the target students attending schools in the wealthier areas compared to the other areas. (This checks for the effect of the two sides of the track on vulnerable students.)
- Schools in tiers 3 and 4 will make greater achievement jumps with focus students than will schools in the lower tiers. (This will tell whether the support provided in accordance with the equity mapping had the desired effect of accelerating results for schools in most need of support.)

Define the Acceptable Floor

The next action step is a punch in the equity stomach. We are still not ready to implement anything until we get agreement on the following question: What are the conditions that are not acceptable under any circumstance?

It is hard to imagine that educators could disagree on what is simply not acceptable, never, ever, no way, no how! But this is the case more often than not. Educators come from different backgrounds, have different training and experience, and have been acculturated by the schools and districts where we have worked. As a result, clarity on what exactly rises to the level of a call to the superintendent with an SOS is too often lacking.

Roy tripped on this live wire when he asked the district office about Sun Middle School (SMS), the school at the top of the equity map identified as most in need of support. SMS was located in the higher poverty area of the district and had seven hundred students, mostly Latino, with 20 percent African American and 10 percent Native American. The school was under-performing, at about 30 percent proficiency on state exams, but African American and Native American achievement was even lower, at about 15 percent.

To craft a support plan that would set up the conditions necessary for the school to thrive, Roy realized that the descriptions of the severity of the school's needs ranged greatly among the district office team. While the team agreed that the school was the most in need of support, the degree of urgency was not a common understanding. This was true even though the district office team was generally conscientious about visiting the schools on a regular basis.

Roy decided to take the team members to visit the school as a group. They planned to walk through classrooms, the guidance office, the yard, and the main office. Roy reminded them to look for any "Not on My Watch!" (NOMW) conditions by answering the following questions:

- Are there any practices that we simply cannot live with and that must be addressed immediately as a district office?
- Are there any practices that violate the equity culture the district is culti-vating?

NOT ON MY WATCH?

The truth about what actually happened on this walk hit Roy very hard and is difficult to share here. In the first hour of the walk, he observed a number of NOMW practices that infuriated him beyond measure. As he looked over at the team, however, an individual or two might scowl at something, but never did anyone say, "Stop! This is not acceptable. Not on my watch!" In fact, when problematic practices were noticed at all, other team members seemed to jump in to explain them away, provide context, or otherwise diminish the severity of the observation.

Here are the actual NOMW practices that Roy saw in the first two hours, none of which were called out by the team. Be advised that these are very painful practices to share and to read about.

Go to the Back of the Room

At the back of every classroom was a table where students worked independently, not involved in the teacher's lesson. In almost every case, the students at the table were African American or Native American boys. Roy asked the principal about this and learned that the school had decided on this system as an incentive to encourage students to turn in homework.

If students did not return homework to class, they were assigned to the back table until they completed it. If they finished the homework, they could rejoin the class midway through the lesson. In some rooms, the back table was quiet, with students working on homework, listening to music on their earbuds, or sleeping. In others, the students were playing hand games, joking, poking one another, or otherwise not in academic mode. This practice was staff suggested and principal approved.

Do as I Say

In one math class, the teacher was giving a lesson at the front of the classroom. Students were in rows. The teacher's voice was unusually loud and her tone sounded harsh and punitive, even when she was not reprimanding anyone. Her voice could be heard several classrooms away as the team approached the class.

The students had their notebooks, all organized the same way, clearly following the teacher's specific guidelines. However, students were not writing anything. The teacher demonstrated how to work algebra problems by solving them on the whiteboard with her back to the students for extended periods of time. It was clear that student questions were not part of the class routine.

At one point when the teacher turned her back to the class, one Native American girl quickly scribbled something in her notebook. She looked very nervous and seemed like she was writing very lightly so as not to call attention to the sound of her pencil. Just then, the teacher turned around and saw her writing. The teacher yelled so loudly that even Roy flinched.

The teacher stomped down the aisle and demanded that the girl put her pencil down, close her notebook, and put her head on the desk. The girl looked so fearful that Roy's eyes turned red. Roy looked at the district team, some of whom walked out of the room at that moment, later saying they felt like they were intruding on a private student-teacher exchange. The rest looked stoic.

Remember that the principal was on the walk as well. Roy fully expected that he, at least, would react and intervene. He did not. When Roy asked him to step outside and explain what he had just seen, the principal said that he had been working with the teacher and that she was improving. Roy went back into the room and asked the girl to show him what she had written. She lifted her head with tearful eyes, and showed him. "Notes," she whispered, and then put her head back down.

Other Duties as Assigned

As the team left that classroom, it was clear to Roy that the district had not calibrated on what constituted an acceptable floor. The principal got a call and left the group at that point. Just then, Roy noticed people with brooms, garbage bins, and dustpans who were standing by the stairwell. He walked over to find a group of five boys (three African American, one Native American, and one Latino) chatting it up under the stairs—during class time.

Roy greeted them and asked what they were doing. "We have to clean here," they said, with an embarrassed expression. When he asked what classes they were assigned to right now, he learned that they had a variety of classes at that time, including English, math, and Spanish. "Who told you to do this right now?" he asked. The boys explained that they had left their trash on the lunch tables the week before, and so, as punishment, the custodian required them to clean during fourth period (after lunch) for the entire week.

"Where are the custodians?" Roy asked.

"We don't know," the boys answered. "Every day we meet them here, they have us get the equipment, then we don't see them again."

Roy looked for the custodians and could not find them anywhere on the grounds; the students were both missing class and unsupervised.

NO! NOT ON MY WATCH!

For some readers, these incidents may seem extreme and impossible. For others, they may represent daily reality. Rest assured that, as with every example in this book, these actually occurred—and things like this occur all over the country every day, largely unchallenged and left to continue. More often than not, they happen in schools where certain groups of students have weak advocacy, often those from low-income homes and students of color.

Are there practices that are simply *not* true, right, or just, and cannot wait to go through a rich, collaborative process to be addressed? Absolutely! Roy rightly identified these three observations as NOMW situations and modeled appropriate action. Here is what he did:

- First, Roy told the principal, assistant principal, and school counselor to go with him to the math class. Roy walked into the room and asked the teacher to step outside while the assistant principal took over the class. The teacher was directed to go to the office, where a conference would occur in the next few minutes. The human resource officer was on the way from the district, and the teachers association representative was advised to attend the conference.
- Roy then walked over to the girl in math class, whose head was now up. He asked her to bring her things and step outside with him, where the counselor met her. Already briefed by phone, the counselor walked the girl to her office to assess her condition and to inform her parents of the incident. Roy directed the administrators who had witnessed the incident to write it up and submit it, along with the counselor's assessment, to the superintendent by the end of that day. This resulted in disciplinary action and a call to Child Protective Services.
- Immediately after his brief conversation with the boys in the stairwell, Roy directed them to leave the custodial equipment where it lay and to go directly to class. They were worried about leaving their assignment, but Roy guaranteed them he would make it all right. As they left, he reminded them of the importance of their education and that they should never be afraid to fight for their schooling. He called a yard supervisor over to walk the boys to class to ensure that their teachers welcomed them into class.
- Then Roy called the director of maintenance and operations and requested his presence at a meeting with the principal and the custodian to establish the clear expectation that students would never again be pulled out of class like this and *never* would they be punished with custodial duties. This meeting was held before the end of that school day.

The lesson here is that a profound key to cultivating an equity culture is that everyone who constitutes the organization must be clear about the nonnegotiables, especially with regard to equity issues. This must be understood for all areas of schools and districts, including issues related to teaching, learning, discipline, supervision, basic human respect, and everything else that defines an organizational culture.

Is the acceptable floor crystal clear in your school or district? Until agreement on NOMW issues is reached, implementation of an equity plan cannot begin because the conditions are not yet set to begin true equity work.

Celebrate Constellations

The next step in setting equity-fertile conditions is to align risks and rewards in a way that celebrate constellations rather than individual bright spots; that is, a clear indicator of an equity culture is that team successes are highly valued. We know that collective equity muscle is the engine that powers equity-centered leaders to disrupt inequities. It stands to reason, then, that leaders must ensure that the value of strong teams permeates the organization.

One truth is that an organization is only as strong as its weakest link. In education this is true for student teams, teacher teams, counselor teams, principal teams, district office teams, boards of education, and the like. Calling a team *weak* is not a personal castigation of any individual; rather, the strength of a team is assessed by its "team-ness," the ability of the group to focus on an equity outcome and to collaborate on implementing an action plan as a cohesive, mutually supportive group.

For example, at Luna Elementary School, at the tier 1 bottom level of the equity map in figure 7.1, achievement was strong for targeted students across the school. However, the fifth-grade teacher team, comprised of some of the most experienced and effective teachers, was also the least cohesive team. As a result, the fifth-grade achievement profile for focus students was consistently lower than that of other grades. Until the fifth-grade team became stronger, fifth-grade results always brought the entire school profile down. *You are as strong as your weakest team.*

Table 7.2. Sample Progress Monitoring Design for Native School District

Desired Equity Goal	Checkpoint 1 (Oct.)	Checkpoint 2 (Dec.)	Checkpoint 3 (Feb.)	Checkpoint 4 (April)	End of Year (June)
Decrease Achievement Gap for Focus Students vs. Others	Benchmark Assessment Data—Unit 1	Benchmark Assessment Data—Unit 2	Benchmark Assessment Data—Unit 3	Benchmark Assessment Data—Unit 4	State Assessment
Similar Achievement of Focus Students Whether They Attend	Benchmark Assessment Data—Unit 1	Benchmark Assessment Data—Unit 2	Benchmark Assessment Data—Unit 3	Benchmark Assessment Data—Unit 4	State Assessment
Schools in Higher-Wealth vs. Higher-Poverty Neighborhoods	*Disaggregate by Neighborhood*	*Disaggregate by Neighborhood*	*Disaggregate by Neighborhood*	*Disaggregate by Neighborhood*	*Disaggregate by Neighborhood*
Accelerate the Growth Rate of Schools in Higher Tiers	Benchmark Assessment Data—Unit 1	Benchmark Assessment Data—Unit 2	Benchmark Assessment Data—Unit 3	Benchmark Assessment Data—Unit 4	State Assessment
	Disaggregate by Tier	*Disaggregate by Tier*	*Disaggregate by Tier*	*Disaggregate by Tier*	*Disaggregated by Tier*

Create a Progress Monitoring Design

The final step in setting conditions prior to engaging in deep equity work is to create a progress monitoring system that will provide frequent feedback about how well the plan is achieving the desired effects. Recall the discussion about defining desired equity outcomes earlier in this chapter. For each desired outcome, design a progress check with enough frequency that tweaks and refinements to the plans can be made in short increments of time to accelerate results. Table 7.2 is an example of a progress monitoring system that should be crafted *prior* to implementing an equity plan.

EQUITY HOOK: A STAR DOES NOT A CONSTELLATION MAKE

SUMMARY

This chapter focuses on the value of cultivating collaborative teams when addressing educational equity issues. In this example, Roy, the district administrator, used the Equity Hook "a star does not a constellation make" to help communicate the need to move away from celebrating isolated bright-spot successes to rewarding team efforts that strengthen the entire system. We have argued that bright spots, by definition, are a sign of an inequitable system because individual successes mean that other parts of the school or district are not as strong.

In this chapter, we presented a process that can help leaders cultivate the equity culture that serves as a basic condition needed for equity work to have real impact on students. In addition, we highlight the need for educators in a school or district to agree on an equity floor: that is, practices that simply cannot be accepted under any circumstance—practices that should make leaders say, "Not on my watch!" We suggest that, sadly, no common agreement exists from what is out-of-bounds in schools, and that what is acceptable is often different depending on the demographics of students who attend the school. This is the very definition of inequity.

Are there practices that violate the equity culture the district is cultivating? In this chapter we described a couple of heart-wrenching true examples of what happens in some schools that should make us all scream, "Not on my watch!" We then modeled what steps the school and district administrators used to confront and resolve them, stressing that a profound key to cultivating an equity culture is that everyone who constitutes the organization must be clear about what is nonnegotiable.

It is important in equity work that we celebrate constellations rather than single stars, that strong teams are valued, and that collective equity muscle is the engine that powers us to disrupt inequities.

EQUITY CONCEPTS

- *Equity Culture:* This is an organizational identity defined by the widespread shared values and common behaviors associated with championing equitable outcomes for students. This requires that we encourage and reward equity—the charge that under the right conditions, every part of a system is uplifted and disparities between parts of a system are reduced.
- *Collective Equity Muscle:* This is the magnified power of equity-centered leadership when an equity culture becomes the norm.

EQUITY ACTIONS

- Take an equity inventory. Take stock of the present equity realities by taking an equity inventory. The easiest way to do this is to identify the stars and then contrast them with the non-stars.
- Create an equity map. Create a pyramid-shaped graphic that tiers units of a school system based on an agreed-upon set of criteria, from those needing less support (tiers 1 and 2, at the bottom) to those requiring more support (tiers 3 and 4, at the top) to get to equity goals.
- Define equitable outcomes. How will you know success when you get there? Decide what the equity outcomes are that you want to see that are not currently part of the current reality.
- Decide the acceptable floor. Determine what the line is that characterizes a condition that is not acceptable under any circumstance.
- Celebrate constellations. Align risks and rewards in a way that celebrates constellations rather than individual accomplishments to cultivate an equity culture.
- Create a progress monitoring system. Design a monitoring system that will provide frequent feedback about how well the plan is having the desired effect. For each desired equity outcome, design a progress check with enough frequency that tweaks and refinements to the plans can be made in time to accelerate results prior to the end of the school year.

Part III

What Are the Most Common
Threats to Equity Leadership?

Chapter Eight

Self-Imposed Equity Hurdles

Equity Hook: Get Out of Your Own Way

Have you ever wondered . . .

- What are the most common mistakes that aspiring equity leaders make?

A team of twelve experienced educational leaders with success as equity leaders formed a team devoted to helping other like-minded educators grow as equity leaders. Each member had experience as a teacher, site leader, and district administrator prior to leaving their districts to join the group. To mark the twentieth anniversary of the group, this highly energized team got together for dinner to reflect on their collective experience.

The founder of the team had mentored each member while in his or her school and district, so each team member had demonstrated the ability to apply equity principles and make profound changes for school systems that directly impacted students. Team members led actions that accelerated growth for the most underserved students in their schools and districts on a host of outcomes. Over those twenty years, the organization had worked in K–12 settings with dozens of districts and hundreds of schools, serving thousands of students. During that time, the team had seen much, laughed many times, cried a fair amount, and definitely learned a lot.

Given their treasure trove of experience addressing educational equity, the team members decided they owed themselves and the field a retrospective on the question most frequently asked at the initial introduction with their school and district partners. Almost immediately after saying, "Hello, I am excited to be your equity thought-partner," they were asked, "What am I doing wrong?" Of course, the polite response was to say something like, "I'm sure it's not something you are doing. Addressing systemic inequities in education is a complex prospect. Yadda, yadda, yadda."

However, the deep and wide experience of the team members led to a different, less polite answer that eventually gave birth to this chapter's Equity Hook: "get out of your own way"! Even though many structural inequities in schools result from legacy practices, some inequities are created because of leaders' actions or inactions. There exists a short list of missteps—dare we say *mistakes*—that leaders make that create conditions in which inequitable practices are even more difficult to correct.

This chapter describes the most common mistakes that directly answer the question, "What am I doing wrong?" As you read, be brave and ask yourself whether you have ever seen or been a part of making any of the errors described below. Be clear. The net result of making these mistakes is the strengthening of the educational glass ceiling, making it harder to break through.

MISTAKE #1: MORE IS BETTER

One of the most common mistakes is the decision to "fix" inequities by adding more programs and initiatives. Sometimes referred to as the Christmas Tree Effect (lots of decorations, no deep roots; Bryk, Easton, Kerbow, Rollow, & Sebring, 1993), this can take several forms.

More Tinkering

An example: Struggling Elementary School is a one-thousand-student school in an impoverished urban area and has been persistently low performing for decades. In 2006, only 12 percent of its students were on grade level in any subject. Fed up, the new board of education demanded reform, and, in lieu of closing the school, gave school teams or other community entities an opportunity to submit school transformation proposals. The team submitting a plan with the greatest chance of turning the school around would gain control of the school.

One community team proposed changing the school calendar from year-round to traditional. Another team wanted to impose school uniforms. A school proposal asked for parent literacy classes. A submission on behalf of the teachers association was to change the composition and meeting schedules of the professional learning communities (collaborative teacher teams) on campus. A final submission included breaking the school into two smaller schools to create a more nurturing learning environment.

After considerable public debate over the span of about eight months regarding which proposal had the best chance for success, the board president observed something profound. "While each proposal has merit," she said, "none deals directly with issues central to teaching and learning. All of the suggested 'reforms' are nice, but none is focused and targeted on drastically improving the poor instructional conditions at the school, a situation that resulted from years of weak leadership." The result was high teacher turnover and a district practice of transferring struggling staff to this site, where parents were not very vocal. This was the elephant in the room that was not part of polite public discourse when discussing the school.

As a result of the board president's courageous stance, no proposal was accepted, and the school board reconsidered its intervention plan. This "more tinkering around the edges" approach stems from a lack of solid understanding of structural inequities in educational systems. It also comes from a place of desperation and frustration that is the result of not knowing how to proceed. As one principal asked as he struggled with this, "Isn't doing *something* better than doing *nothing*?" The answer is no. Adding decorations without addressing core issues takes human and financial resources away from the True North.

More Programs

Educators often become program shoppers, looking for the silver bullet that will create the needed change. One high school principal, Trina, complained that after years of such shopping, there were so many programs in her school that she could not keep up with them. Trina was constantly calling substitutes to stand in for teachers going through new training programs. Although all the programs had the greatest of intentions, she was not sure specifically what each was supposed to achieve, how, and for which students.

There seemed to be overlap in many of the goals and activities, but the teachers involved in the different initiatives rarely communicated, much less collaborated. There existed a fragmentation of efforts. Frankly, Trina felt that many of the programs had been forced on her by central administration, staff, or the community. She wished the school could focus in more depth on improvement efforts that had already begun before adding new programs.

A colleague asked her, "Why don't you just say that you don't want any more programs?" Her reply was, "Oh, I can't do that. I am fearful that people would think that I don't want to improve my school!" Still, Trina wondered whether there was any way to determine which programs were best for her school and which were not particularly effective.

Subsequently, she and some staff members attended an institute with their equity thought-partners where they were challenged to analyze the disparate programs at their school, especially those they considered interventions for struggling students. Most often, interventions were the brainchild of someone on staff or in the district who identified a problem and proposed a quick solution, often to satisfy adult interests. Trina realized it was the first time in a while that she had been encouraged to think solely in terms of what was best for her students.

With the assistance of her data team, Trina began analyzing program impact at the school, becoming familiar with all the efforts, collecting data, and finding out how others—including students and parents—evaluated the programs.

Some of the findings from the team included the following:

- *ISD Class.* This detention class kept students who were tardy out of class for a whole period. During that time, no academic work was given or expected to be completed. No provisions were made for missed academic work. What's more, no one could remember what ISD stood for because the program was so old!
- *Academic Study Hall.* This class was a consequence for students who did not turn in homework. It was a mandatory elective to help students complete homework and to receive academic assistance with concepts and test preparation. There was no guidance for the teacher, little collaboration with the students' teachers, and no evidence that this period had any impact on student achievement.
- *Double Periods.* This structure was designed to give students extra math periods. Because it cut across the lunch period, many students cut class and went unnoticed as they blended into the crowds in the lunch area. There was no mechanism for monitoring attendance or effectiveness.
- *College Preparatory Programs.* Many programs labeled "college prep" had a remedial label until the district eliminated remedial courses. However, the course content in the formerly remedial classes did not change. Expectations for achievement and behavior varied from teacher to teacher.
- *English Learner Programs.* Separate classes were offered for EL students. Classes included new arrivals and long-term EL students. The curriculum was below grade level and not aligned to the English proficiency levels of students.

The team identified many more programs and initiatives. The epiphany was that the school simply did not have the capacity to implement and monitor with technical soundness all the specialized interventions and programs it offered. This is initiative overload, plain and simple (Fullan & Quinn, 2015)! While the intent to serve students is commendable, the sheer number of efforts is impossible to manage and monitor to ensure quality.

Here is a hard leadership challenge: Equity leaders must learn to say no to yet another wonderful idea! While easy to say, experience shows that this is very difficult to do, but we must do this if we are to set the conditions necessary for deep equity work to take root and make a difference for students.

MISTAKE #2: EVERYBODY KNOWS

Countless systemic failures are exacerbated by leaders who take action based on what "everybody knows." These assumptions seep into the system and are accepted as truths and not challenged. This phenomenon occurs when decisions are made without adequately studying issues, peeling back data, applying an equity lens, and deeply understanding equity conditions.

For example, "everybody knows" that:

- struggling students should be retained to help give them more time to catch up;
- grades are the best, most objective criteria for determining program placement;
- struggling students should be offered simpler classes so that they can be more academically successful; and
- students with disabilities need to be taught basic skills rather than core grade-level curriculum.

In fact, each of these statements runs counter to much of the evidence, and systems based on these beliefs serve to exacerbate existing inequities. Table 8.1 provides research-based responses to each of the statements that everybody knows.

The point is that many times what everybody knows is simply not accurate, especially with regard to long-standing inequitable practices. Taking action based on faulty assumptions worsens systems and results in very different outcomes for students. As vigilant equity stewards, we must ensure that such assumptions are challenged and tested before moving ahead with action that affect students' futures. And if we are unsure about the veracity of the assumptions, we must ask someone who is knowledgeable and credible. Remember, this work must be done by constellations!

MISTAKE #3: NORMALIZING FAILURE

Normalizing failure is another common systemic condition in schools and districts. The normalization of failure occurs when the lack of success of an individual or group of students occurs over time and becomes accepted as the status quo (Johnson & Avelar La Salle, 2010; Noguera &Wing, 2008). Equity advocates please beware: It is possible for this to be an unconscious phenomenon that happens without any intention of it becoming institutionalized.

One thing is clear. If the Equity True North is not front and center in the attention of the leader, then inequities become invisible and are not ad-

Table 8.1. Research-Based Responses to Commonly Held Misperceptions

"Everybody Knows" Belief	*Research-Based Response*	*Citation*
Struggling students should be retained to help give them more time to catch up: Giving students another year of the same has not proven effective.	Retained students are among the largest group of dropouts.	Flores-Gonzalez 2002; Haney et al., 2004; National Association of School Psychologists, 2003
Grades are the best, most objective criteria for program placement.	Grades are extremely subjective in most cases, not usually calibrated from teacher to teacher, even if they teach the same subject and grade. When test scores are compared with grades students receive, an A in a low-income school would be a C in a high-income school. Therefore, attaching high stakes, such as placement in premium or lesser pathways, to grades is highly objectionable and unreliable.	Abt Associates (cited in Johnson, 2002); McMillan, 2005

"Everybody Knows" Belief	Research-Based Response	Citation
Struggling students should be offered simpler classes so that they can be more academically successful.	Offering simpler classes for struggling students rarely accelerates growth. Our extensive experience in schools indicates that students in homogeneous lower-level classes experience the greatest degree of failure by almost every measure, including grades and test scores. Further, years in this lower track put students further and further behind. On a related point, schools need to assess whether low-level content is masquerading as being on grade level or college preparatory when it is in fact below grade level. When this happens, we are setting students up for academic ridicule by making them less academically competitive.	Tierney, Corwin & Colyar, 2004; Barton & Coley, 2009; Johnson, 2002; Oakes, 2005
Students with disabilities need to be taught basic skills rather than core grade-level curriculum.	Students with disabilities include a huge range of cognitive and academic levels. Most could receive educational benefits from core curriculum if presented with appropriate differentiated strategies.	Harry & Klingner, 2006

dressed. This is actually a function of how the brain works. As a survival mechanism, the human brain makes unconscious decisions about what to put in the foreground and what to relegate to background.

For another attention example: Can you see your nose right now. No? What about now? Yes? Actually, your noses are always visible, yet your brain ignores it for more interesting stimuli. (This is true unless, of course, a teenager has a pimple on his nose the morning before the prom. His brain *will* have him see his nose all day long!)

The point is simply that a common mistake is to push pause on the equity button in favor of other priorities. That very act—conscious or not—severely limits educational equity for students. How do we keep the equity focus when so many other issues compete for attention? By building collective equity muscle. By working as part of an equity constellation. In other words, by developing an equity culture and being surrounded by mission-aligned colleagues, leaders support one another in remaining disciplined in order to stay the equity course.

MISTAKE #4: TRUSTING WITHOUT VERIFYING

"Trust but verify" is a Russian proverb that perfectly describes the remedy to the next most common mistake. Often, equity leaders are so emotionally connected to the true, right, and just cause that they make the mistake of assuming that initiatives, programs, and practices will be fully supported and implemented by design—until we find they are not.

The tip is to remember that if you expect it, you must inspect it. This is not because leaders are power mongers or micromanagers. It is because major consequences exist for students when we fail to closely monitor to see if our good intentions actually bear equity fruit. Table 8.2 lists some common initiatives and the dangerous unintended consequences that can occur when we fail to inspect what we expect.

MISTAKE #5: PRIORITIZING ADULT INTERESTS

One final area where leaders make frequent errors, and where the public rhetoric and private talk differ greatly, is in prioritizing adult interests. Rarely do members of the education community—including teachers, administrators, parents, students, and community members—openly admit that some systems are designed to satisfy adult interests at the expense of student success. This mere suggestion would set some people into a defensive tizzy!

Maybe some educators have never thought about the notion that adult interests often override student needs. We suspect, however, that many readers will relate to some of the following examples from on-the-ground work in schools and districts that make it difficult to claim that it doesn't exist.

One low-performing middle school decided to become a math and science magnet school for the district. Teachers, administrators, parents, and students wanted to increase the rigor and reputation of their school and orient their students toward careers of the future, many of which involve math and science. A master schedule was developed, replete with challenging math, science, history, and English classes. Electives included preview-review classes to accompany core classes for struggling students, as well as engag-

Table 8.2. Potential Unintended Consequences of Equity Reforms

Examples of Reform Initiatives and Policies	*Intended Outcome*	*Potential Unintended Consequence*
Class-Size Reduction	To lower the student-teacher ratio	To fill the staffing demands, more classrooms may be staffed with unqualified teachers. Also, the need for additional facilities may result in classes being taught in less-than-ideal spaces (cafeterias, shared classes, even hallways).
High School Houses/ Academies/Small Learning Communities/ "Small Schools"	To create smaller, more personalized learning communities on high school campuses	This structure can lead to tracking and segregation of student groups. A typical scenario results in student electives (such as band, athletics, spirit groups), rather than other educational criteria, determining house placement. This has serious implications for student placement.

For example, generally, athletes and spirit groups take their electives at the end of the day so that their practices can extend beyond the school day. Students cannot participate in extra-curricular programs unless they meet satisfactory academic achievement criteria.

Therefore, placing those students in the same house results in one grouping of students that are the most involved, successful students. Other houses may, for the same reason, contain all the honors or AP students. By default, at least one house will generally contain more of the students who are not "connected" to school and who are not as academically successful.

As one student interview revealed, "Some houses are the 'in-houses' and that one is the 'out-house'!" |

Examples of Reform Initiatives and Policies	Intended Outcome	Potential Unintended Consequence
Block Scheduling	To provide secondary students with additional time to participate in each learning period	Teachers who are not skilled at teaching "bell to bell" in a traditional fifty-minute period are even less successful at effectively executing lessons for longer time periods (as much as an hour longer). Given the fact that remedial and lower-level classes are often assigned to less experienced teachers, struggling students in blocked periods can experience most of an entire day in settings where, for long periods of time, little productive learning occurs.
Eliminating Remedial and Low-Level Classes	To align instruction to rigorous academic content and performance standards and increase expectations for student achievement levels	More students than ever can fail under such a system if the necessary interventions (such as teacher training to address differentiated instruction or providing extra instructional time) are not in place to provide struggling students with needed scaffolding and support in order for them to achieve. Course rigor may be compromised and watered down.
Frequent Formative Assessments Administered to Students	To provide teachers and administrators with incremental feedback on the effectiveness of the instructional program for individual students so that tailored modifications can be designed based on those data	Assessments can become so time consuming that teachers sacrifice a significant amount of potential teaching time to complete assessments. This problem is exacerbated if assessments are administered in a one-on-one student-to-teacher setting, resulting in the majority of the class doing busywork for extended periods of time while individual assessments take place. The problem is worse when teachers focus on the administration of the assessments and not the meaning behind the data that results from the assessments.
Restorative Disciplinary Practice	To address the school-to-prison patterns stemming from disproportionate punishment for poor students and students of color	If not properly implemented, school staff can perceive the initiative as a move prohibiting all disciplining of students. As a result, student misconduct and a disorderly school culture may become the norm, creating a situation where teachers and site administrators feel disempowered to address poor behavior.

Examples of Reform Initiatives and Policies	Intended Outcome	Potential Unintended Consequence
Homeroom/ Study Hall	To provide students with time during the day to do homework, read, organize their materials, or orient themselves as students	If not properly implemented, students can have extended periods of wasted time (often between fifteen minutes to more than an hour, depending on the school). Struggling students, especially, can become disengaged, filling the time with a host of unproductive activities. Often, these minutes are defined as "noninstructional" by contractual agreement with teachers' associations, severely limiting the types of experiences for students. That time is often limited to activities that do not require teachers to have to plan. This reduces the amount of available time for powerful instruction and promotes a climate of laxness and low expectations.
Professional Learning Communities (PLCs)	To provide educators with a process of engaging in collaborative inquiry and professional growth with the ultimate aim of improving educational opportunity for students	The intent of the professional learning community can be lost to the rules and structures surrounding it and can result in no tangible benefit to students. PLCs can deteriorate into a synonym for "meeting," as in the phrase, "We PLC every Tuesday." Sometimes it can connote meetings with specific rules, such as: administrators may not direct the agendas, only team members may attend, they must occur during the contract day, only two PLCs can be held a month, and so on. Absent clear school- or districtwide academic targets or strong leadership, "PLC time" can translate into systemic nonproductive time.

ing math and science application classes, such as rocketry and pre-engineering. Students were at the heart of program development, except in one situation.

A Moral Dilemma

While most teachers either held multiple subjects or subject-specific credentials in core subjects, one teacher on staff still held an old, rare vocational credential. He was hired when school needs were different. For the past eighteen years, the master schedule had been developed to include five sections of shop class to fill his assignment. The design team was perplexed about how to plan his assignment with the change in emphasis for the school.

Additional troubling data included the number of students who needed preview-review companion classes of core classes to be able to compete in rigorous courses. The school needed effective teachers to teach sections of the preview-review course. Only the vocational education teacher was left unassigned by credentialing restrictions and could not teach anything but his subject.

The design team was clear that they needed multiple subject teachers or subject specialists to teach the support classes to offer the struggling students support for advanced courses. Absent this support, students would most certainly continue to flounder. The design team saw how miserably the neighboring school did when it put all eighth-graders into algebra without any instructional differentiation or extra support. They could not in good conscience put low-performing students in higher-level classes without providing them with the necessary support.

The entire premise of the magnet was that, if given proper supports, all students could access the highest levels of curriculum. The design team was clear on the student need, but the principal explained that he had to discuss certain staffing issues with the district. After several days, the principal reported that the district could not add a teacher to the staffing ratio, so the team was directed to create assignments for all existing teachers.

Though the teachers' contract allowed for teacher transfers based on program need, this had never been done before, and the district did not feel comfortable pursuing that path. Many difficult discussions later, the design team was forced to assign five sections of students to the vocational class, thereby reducing core support class opportunities for students. As a consequence, five sections of lower-level core course options were created for struggling students, who were therefore unable to take the support class. When school reopened, 150 students did not partake of the premium program offered at the school.

Educators are all too accustomed to situations such as this, where adult interests override student needs, though few will speak of it publicly. Of course, we are not naive to the complexity of how system components interact and the dynamic of the human business in which we are engaged. However, it is important to ask:

- Are these practices equally applied in all neighborhoods, equally affecting all students?
- Are they ever acceptable?
- What role should adult interests have in school and district decisions that affect students?

- How should a school system appropriately handle adult interests such as the one in the scenario?
- Do we have the will to speak up and shout out what is right for students who are being underserved?

At what point do we draw a collective line in the sand and admit that all systems, even failing ones, are perfectly built to get the results they are getting? Rather than blaming students, parents, or society for poor academic achievement by large groups of students, let us take a critical look at our behaviors; at who is valued in our systems; at decisions we make about structures, policies, and practices; and at the underlying belief systems to determine if anything within our sphere of influence might be a help or hindrance to equity and academic achievement for all students.

As one district director responded when challenged by a school about the need to address parent and community deficits, "When we have done everything we know to do that is within our total control as educators and student success has plateaued, then I will personally walk across the street and start knocking on doors. Have we done everything we know to do?"

EQUITY HOOK: GET OUT OF YOUR OWN WAY

SUMMARY

- Mistake #1: More Is Better. This is the very common misconception that struggling students could improve if schools and district just had enough programs for them; aka, the Christmas Tree Effect (many decorations, shallow or no roots).

  - More Tinkering: This is when leaders implement programs or participate initiatives that only tangentially relate to student needs.
  - More Programs: This occurs when leaders layer one program or initiative atop another until they exceed the capacity of the staff to implement them with any depth.

- Mistake #2: Everybody Knows. This is when leaders accept conventional wisdom without challenge when crafting equity plans. The risk is that what everybody knows is not substantiated by evidence and that poor decisions or mistakes are made as a result.
- Mistake #3: Normalization of Failure. This occurs when leaders do not use their equity vision as their guide. Leaders stop noticing failure that may exist in every form (teaching, learning, facilities, discipline, etc.) because it is so prevalent that it goes unchallenged.

- Mistake #4: Trusting without Verifying. Leaders often expect their equity vision to be implemented as they see it in their mind's eye. They launch initiatives and never cycle back to monitor the quality of implementation.
- Mistake #5: Prioritizing Adult Interests. This is the ugly elephant in the room. Leaders may accept the tension between the Equity True North and practical school system realities. As a result, leaders may not challenge situations where adult interests override student needs.

Conclusion

Make Educational Equity Your True North

Equity Hook: Do You Want to *Be* Right or *Do* Right?

The fact that you were compelled to pick up this book and read it to the conclusion suggests some characteristics that are probably true about you:

- You do *not* accept that demographics should determine destiny.
- You care deeply about providing equitable access and the opportunity for high-quality education to *every* student.
- You believe that equity is the True North that should guide school and district policies, practices, and decisions.
- You are disturbed by what you see as a system that advantages some students and disadvantages others based on issues over which students have no control.
- You are an equity leader.
- You wonder why there are not more equity leaders.

While equity leaders often feel alone, the truth is that there exists a large community of educators with equity heart. All schools and districts have people who champion the cause of educational equity. They might be principals or other site administrators, central office administrators, teachers, counselors, coaches, other support staff members, or board of education or community members.

If it is true that a large community of equity leaders exists, where are they? And why do inequitable systems in schools and districts still exist? Underlying the complexity of this question is one basic truth: There are three prerequisites to leading meaningful advances in educational equity. Figure C.1 illustrates a continuum of equity leadership development. For equity to take root, leaders must move through all three stages. Many leaders start their quest to follow an Equity True North at the beginning, but fewer are able to satisfy the other prerequisites.

Ask yourself the following questions to see where you are on the continuum.

EQUITY HEART

- Did you experience an emotional or physical reaction to the story of Kyle in the preface?
- Did you become saddened or angry about all the Kyles you have known over the years?
- Do you feel passionately that demographics do *not* have to determine destiny?
- Are you frustrated by policies and practices in your school or district that you know produce inequitable outcomes for students?
- Do you often find yourself in disbelief that everyone does not see inequitable practices that you see with your equity vision?
- Does the Inevitability Assumption that some students just are not going to reach high levels of success in school make you crazy?
- Do you become offended when you observe the normalization of failure in practice?
- Are you confident in your belief in educational equity, especially for our most vulnerable students? *Do you know you are right about this?*

THE WILL TO ACT

- Do you feel compelled to do something to address inequitable systems?
- Are you upset when people discuss equity issues but take no helpful action?
- Have tried to address equity issues in the past?

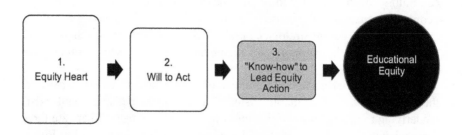

Figure C.1. Protocol for Peeling Back the Wallpaper

- Regardless of your job title, do you see yourself as an equity leader with a moral imperative to correct the legacy of inequitable school systems?
- Do you feel you have the passion and energy to take equity action?
- Are you sick and tired of being sick and tired of the present state of inequitable systems?
- Are you confident that your desire to correct inequitable systems is the true, right, and just thing to do? *Do you know you are right about this?*

These questions demonstrate that the will to act requires more than empathizing with the plight of vulnerable students. After honest reflection, some educators will say that this is the professional next step they are working toward.

THE KNOW-HOW TO LEAD EQUITY ACTIONS

This is where progress is made. Leaders at this stage are able to lead changes in adult practice and open up new possibilities for students. This stage requires information, skills, and experience that many educators have yet to fully gain. We may not want to admit this in public, but until we as a community of equity leaders develop the know-how to lead equity efforts, having equity heart and the will to lead changes leaves us "being right." But "doing right" requires leaders to engage in a degree of intentional study and practice.

The aim of this book is to provide you, our beloved equity leadership community, with the know-how to translate your equity heart and your will to lead impactful change into leadership that truly changes lives. In each chapter of this book, equity leaders from across the educational landscape have shared nuanced lessons about how to lead equity work that changes systems and opens up new opportunities for students.

Here is a quiz. As a way to review the major concepts in the book, try to fill in figure C.1. *But do not do it alone.* Instead:

1. Share this book with some colleagues who you think would benefit from the lessons presented here. Be brave and ask people who may not necessarily be equity-inclined to consider joining you in this experience.
2. Individually, try to complete figure C.1 as an exercise to see how well the Equity Hooks trigger your memory of the major takeaways. See what resonated with each of you individually.
3. Then, come together as an equity community and share your notes. Collective equity muscle is strengthened and your own thinking will become clearer processing the know-how presented in the book with

colleagues. This process will also provide a forum for equity leaders in progress to fortify their own thinking. Inviting others who might not consider them equity leaders to the discussion opens up opportunities for them to grow in their equity understanding. It also provides you an opportunity to practice some of the skills for interacting with others shared in the book.

We hope that everyone who reads this book is clear about two major points:

1. *Long-standing patterns of academic struggles for entire demographic groups of students are not the fault of any one person or any one part of the school system.*

   - Is it the teachers' fault? No.
   - The teachers unions' fault? No.
   - Those darn principals? No.
   - Central office administrators? No.
   - It's the board of education, right? No.

   Inequitable student outcomes are no one's fault and everyone's fault, both at the same time. Are there ineffective teachers, self-serving unions, uncaring principals, scattered central office administrators, and crazy boards? Of course there are! If we denied that, we would lose all education street cred.

   But it is both *unhelpful* and *untrue* to blame educational inequities on any one of these entities.

   - It is unhelpful because it alienates and repels the very people who need to be part of the solution. Remember the lessons from each chapter that equity leaders must work *with and through* those very adults to impact the students in need of our urgent attention. We don't just want to *be* right, we want to be able to *do* right.
   - It is also untrue to blame any one entity because school systems are ecosystems; each is a complex network of interacting elements (Barth & Delson, 2015). They are inextricably connected and are deeply interdependent. As much as it would be expedient to ascribe fault to an individual or one part of an educational system, it is simply not accurate.

2. *Disrupting inequitable systems rarely requires completely changing schools and districts.* All of the leaders who shared lessons in these chapters aggressively advanced the cause of educational justice, but they did so from the inside out. They worked within the system, en-

gaged in self-reflection, and facilitated self-discovery in others, demonstrating respect and dignity for the adults who work within the schools and districts with the goal of inspiring as many people as possible from across the system to become an integral part of the solution. Disrupting inequities need not be mean-spirited nor confrontational. Guided by the true, right, and just vision of equity for all rather than a host of other possible motivations, equity leaders can change school and district systems, impact our most vulnerable students, and change entire communities.

We all can and must break through the educational glass ceiling to create equitable systems that ensure that every student receives the excellent education that currently only some receive.
Enough Is Enough.

References

Adelman, C. (1999). *Answers in the toolbox: Academic intensity, attendance patterns, and bachelor's degree attainment.* Washington, DC: US Department of Education.

Avelar La Salle, R., & Johnson, R. S. (2016). Peeling back the wallpaper. *Education Leadership, 7*(3), 79–82.

Avelar La Salle, R., & Johnson, R. S. (February 7, 2018). Are your students on track to success? Questions school and district leaders should be asking. *Education Week, 37*(19), 24–25.

Avelar La Salle, R., Johnson, R., & Maldonado French, L. (October 9, 2014). What can a vaccination study teach educators about transforming schools and districts? *Education Week 34*(7), 22-23.

Barth, R., & Delson, J. (2015). *THINK Together: How YOU can play a role in improving education in America.* Santa Ana, CA: Wheatmark.

Barton, P. E., & Coley, R. J. (2009). *Parsing the achievement gap: Policy information report.* Princeton, NJ: Policy and Evaluation Research Center, Educational Testing Service.

Becker, H. S. (1963). *The outsiders.* New York: Free Press.

Brown v. Board of Education, 347 U.S. 483 (1954). The reported opinions of Judge McCormick and the Ninth Circuit, *Mendez v. Westminster [sic] School Dist. of Orange County,* 64 F. Supp. 544 (S.D. Cal. 1946), aff'd, 161 F.2d 774 (9th Cir. 1947) (en banc).

Bryk, A. S., Easton, J. Q., Kerbow, D., Rollow, S. G., & Sebring, P. A. (1993). *A view from the elementary schools: The state of reform in Chicago.* Chicago: Consortium on Chicago School Research. Retrieved April 26, 2010, from https://consortium.uchicago.edu/sites/default/files/publications/AViewFromTheElementarySchools_TheStateOfReformInChicago.pdf

Fiarman, S. E. (2016). Unconscious bias: When good intentions aren't enough. *Educational Leadership, 74* (3), 10–15.

Flores-Gonzalez, N. (2002). *School kids/street kids.* New York: Teachers College Press.

Ford, D. Y., & Grantham, T. C. (2003). Providing access for culturally diverse gifted students: From deficit to dynamic thinking. *Theory into Practice, 42*(3), 217–25.

Ford, J. E. (2016). The roots of discipline disparity. *Educational Leadership, 74* (3), 42–46.

Fullan, M. (1993). *Change forces: Probing the depths of education reform.* London: Falmer Press.

Fullan, M. (2011). *The moral imperative realized.* Thousand Oaks, CA: Corwin Press.

Fullan, M., & Bush, V. L. (2006). *Coherence: The right drivers in action for schools, districts, and systems.* Thousand Oaks, CA: Corwin.

Gawande, A. (2007). *Better: A surgeon's notes on performance .* New York: Metropolitan Books.

Haney, W., Madaus, G., Abrams, L., Wheelock, A., Miao, J., & Gruia, I. (2004*). The education pipeline in the United States, 1970–2000.* Chestnut Hill, MA: Lynch School of Education, Boston College.

Harry, B., & Klingner, J. (2006). *Why are so many minority students in special education? Understanding race and disability in schools.* New York: Teachers College Press.

Johnson, R. S. (2002). *Using data to close the achievement gap: How to measure equity in our schools.* Thousand Oaks, CA: Corwin Press.

Johnson, R. S., & Avelar La Salle, R. (2010). *Data strategies to uncover and eliminate hidden inequities: The wallpaper effect.* Thousand Oaks, CA: Corwin Press.

Johnson, R. S., & Bush, V. L. (2006). Leading the culturally responsive school. In *F. English (Ed.) Sage Handbook of Education Leadership,* 121-148.

Lee, J., & Wong, K. K. (2004). The impact of accountability on racial and socioeconomic equity: Considering both school resources and achievement outcomes. *American Educational Research Journal, 41*(4), 797–832.

Lindsey, R. B., Graham, S. M., Westphal Jr., R. C., & Jew, C. L. (2008). *Culturally proficient inquiry: A lens for identifying and examining educational gaps.* Thousand Oaks, CA: Corwin Press.

Ma, J., Pender, M., & Welch, M. (2016). *Education pays 2016: The benefits of higher education for individuals and society.* New York: College Board. Retrieved September 25, 2018, from https://trends.collegeboard.org/sites/default/files/education-pays-2016-full-report.pdf

McKinsey & Company. (2009). *The economic impact of the achievement gap in America's schools. McKinsey & Company Social Sector Office,* pp. 1–24. Retrieved April 19, 2010, from https://dropoutprevention.org/wp-content/uploads/2015/07/ACHIEVEMENT_GAP_REPORT_20090512.pdf

McMillan, J. H. (2005). Secondary teachers classroom assessment and grading practices. *Educational Measure Issues and Practices, 20*(1), 20–32.

Menendez, R. (Director). (1998). *Stand and Deliver.* Burbank, CA: Warner Bros.

National Association of School Psychologists. (2003). *Position statement on student grade retention and social promotion.* Retrieved January 8, 2010, from http://www.nasponline.org/about_nasp/pospaper_graderetent.aspx

National Student Clearinghouse Report 2016. https://studentclearinghouse.org/high-schools/studenttracker/

Neal, L. I., McCray, A. D., Webb-Johnson, G. C., & Bridgest, S. T. (2003). The effects of African American movement styles on teachers' perceptions and reactions. *Journal of Special Education, 37*(1), 49–57.

Noguera, P., & Wing, J. Y. (2006). *Unfinished business: Closing the racial achievement gap in our schools.* San Francisco, CA: Jossey-Bass.

Nyhan, B., Reifler, J., Richey, S., & Freed, G. (2014). Effective messages in vaccine promotion: A randomized trial. *Pediatrics, 133*(4), e835–42. doi:10.1542/peds.2013-2365d

Oakes, J. (2005) *Keeping track: How schools structure inequality,* 2nd ed. New Haven, CT: Yale University Press.

O'Connor, C, & DeLuca Fernandez, S. (2006). Race, class, and disproportionality: Reevaluating the relationship between poverty and special education placement. *Educational Researcher, 35,* 6–11.

Olson, L. (2004). Enveloping expectations: Federal law demands that schools teach the same content to children they wrote off a quarter-century ago. *Education Week, 23*(17), 8–20.

Tierney, W. G., Corwin, Z. B., & Colyar, J. E., Eds. (2004). *Preparing for college: Nine elements of effective outreach.* New York: SUNY Education Press.

Index

About the Authors

Robin Avelar La Salle grew up in Echo Park, near downtown Los Angeles. Avelar La Salle holds a PhD in education from Stanford University, with an emphasis on language, literacy, and culture. She taught elementary, middle school, high school, and university students in Southern and Northern California. Avelar La Salle spent years as the administrator for curriculum, staff development, and assessment at a school district outside of Los Angeles. She has held numerous positions in research and consulting focused on advancing academic success for historically underperforming, underserved students. For the past two decades, Avelar La Salle has served as cofounder and chief executive officer for Principal's Exchange (now Orenda Education), a technical support organization and thought partner dedicated to improving schools and districts serving high-poverty, high-minority communities.

Ruth S. Johnson is a professor emeritus at California State University, Los Angeles. She has served in a variety of educational settings in New Jersey and California. Ruth received her EdD in 1985 from Rutgers, The State University of New Jersey. Her dissertation was titled *An Exploratory Study of Academic Labeling, Student Achievement and Student Ethnographic Characteristics*. At the K–12 level, she served as a classroom teacher, an instructional consultant, a director of elementary education, an analyst, an assistant superintendent of schools in the areas of curriculum and business, and superintendent of schools. She has initiated efforts that resulted in raising academic standards and student achievement in low-performing school districts. She served as an education consultant for the New Jersey Department of Education and as a director for two nonprofit organizations in California that focused on raising student achievement in underserved student populations. Her major scholarly interests and publications focus on processes related to changing the academic culture of urban schools, with an emphasis on access and equity. In addition to her four published books, she has written numerous book chapters, articles, editorials, research reports, and manuscript reviews. As a recognized speaker, she has presented nationally to scholarly and professional audiences and serves as a consultant to schools and districts.